❀

The Psychology of Mystical Awakening

Other translations by Swami Savitripriya

Hymn of the Lord
Bhagavad Gita

Nectar of Divine Love
Narada Bhakti Sutras

Necklace of Devotional Gems
Bhaktiratnavali

Cosmic Play of the Goddess
Devi Mahatmayam

Hymn of the Guru
Guru Gita

The Divine Consciousness
Shiva Sutras

The Secret of the Inner Divine Heart-Self
Pratyabhijnahridayam

Universal Manifestation of Divine Consciousness
Vijnanabharava

The Divine Vibration of the Cosmos
Spanda Karikas

A Garland of Gems to Shiva
Shivastotravali

Major Upanishads

Original books by Swami Savitripriya
Kundalini Shakti: From Awakening to Enlightenment
The Worlds of the Chakras
The Faces of the Goddess
Enlightenment in Daily Life
From Darkness to Light: My Autobiography

Psychology
of
Mystical
Awakening

New World Hinduism Volume 1

Patañjali Yoga Sutras

A New World Translation by
Swami Savitripriya

New Life Books

Sunnyvale, California

Psychology of Mystical Awakening: Patañjali Yoga Sutras, A New World Translation by Swami Savitripriya © Copyright 1991 Institute for New Life

Library of Congress Cataloging-in-Publication Data
    Patañjali.
    [Yogasutra. English & Sanskrit]
    The psychology of mystical awakening : a guide for everyday life : a new translation of the Patañjali yoga sutras / by Swami Savitripriya.
        p.   cm.
    English and Sanskrit (Sanskrit in roman).
    Includes index.
    ISBN 1-879722-01-1 : $12.95
    1. Yoga—Early works to 1800.   I. Savitripriya, Swami, 1930–
II. Title.
B132.Y6P267   1991   91-17576
181'.452—dc20   CIP

Table of Contents

Swami Savitripriya

Swami Savitripriya is an American Siddha Guru, a
Master of Shaktipat-Kundalini Yoga, and a nun in the
ancient Smarta Sampradaya monastic order. Her
deep, transcendental understanding of the Hindu
scriptures and solutions to human suffering is the
result of having attained Nirvikalpa Samadhi, the
highest state of God-Realization. Through a thought,
glance, word or touch, she awakens others to the
permanent state of Love and Consciousness that is
their own True-Essence. Swami Savitripriya is a
remarkable blend of East and West. A contemporary
American in tune with today's Western Culture, she
conveys a profound knowledge gained through direct
experience in clear, lucid English, using terms that are
easily understood. Her commonsense, practical
approach to everyday life and spiritual unfoldment
removes the mystery that so often surrounds Eastern
teachings. She has translated more than 20 Hindu
scriptures into modern English with depth and
clarity, and has authored many original books on
spiritual unfoldment. Swami Savitripriya is the
founder of Shiva-Shakti Kashmir Shaivite Ashram
and Monastery, Holy Mountain University, and the
Institute for New Life, a non-profit organization
dedicated to making spiritual life both understand-
able and possible for Westerners in the midst of
modern high-tech society.

Introduction

❀   *T*he most important thing about a translation is not to try and teach the reader another language, but to convey the fullest meaning possible for a word in the context of a particular sentence. Trying to translate any language from one to another, and especially Sanskrit into a language such as English, which has no religious, philosophical or cosmological equivalents, is not the easiest task. In addition, using one English word for one Sanskrit word, as many people have tried to do, is virtually impossible if the translation is to have any real significance. Also, using page after page of scholarly explanations, root analysis and so on in an attempt to explain what the translator usually has no personal knowledge of, is hardly the answer, either. Many people have tried, but rarely with any success. At least this is my experience after trying to make certain to read every English translation that has appeared anywhere in the world. I had hoped to find one that was accurate both in the literal translation of each word, and in the interpretation of the stanza as a whole. In addition, unless one has personally experienced the levels of Consciousness that are described in the Sutras, it would be impossible to know what the stanzas mean. Since I was unable to find a translation that was accurate, I decided to write this translation. Those of you who have read other translations will find this one radically different in almost every way.

Unless we Westerners have been exposed for many years to the highly sophisticated mythology, psychology, philosophy and cosmology of the Hindu tradition, and have been fortunate enough to have been guided by an Enlightened Master towards the direct realization of Transcendental Truth—which can only be gained through transcending the mind and intellect—we will remain bewildered when trying to grasp the full meaning of these pragmatic, life-affirming teachings and finely drawn road maps that are so relevant for today's world. This, combined with the difficulty that Westerners often experience when trying to read and understand an English text written by someone who does not have a contemporary grasp of English, and the difficulty in making sense out of guesses and speculations written by scholars with no personal experience of Mystical Union, was a great motivation for me to write this book in the way I have written it.

For these reasons, I have done my best to translate enough of the underlying, implied meaning of each of the Sutras in a way that would be easily understood, and meaningful, to Westerners and other English speaking people. I decided to assume that most people who would be reading these Sutras would not have any knowledge of Sanskrit, and little, if any, knowledge of the philosophical or cosmological tradition. Since I am quite certain that this is the case, since even such widely used terms as 'meditation', 'enlightenment', 'gunas', 'non-attachment', and many other terms are usually grossly misunderstood, I have written the implied meaning of the word in the context of the Sutra. Thus, while doing my best to refrain from writing commentaries, at the same time I realized that if the Sutras were to be understood, I would need to clearly define the sometimes compound meaning of a single word, or concept. The meanings needed to be understood well enough for people to apply them to daily life, and understand precisely why they should, or should not, do what was being suggested. This resulted in my often times using several words, a sentence, or even long paragraphs to define a word, especially the first time the word appeared. For example, in Chapter One, Sutra 1, I thought it necessary to set the scene, and define the word 'yoga' in terms of its practice, philosophy, psychology, benefits, goal and ultimate result. Otherwise, reading the first sutras as, 'Now yoga instruction', might very well be the first and last a person might want to read. The same applies to Chapter One, Sutra 12, in which the word 'vairagya' first appears. This word is so commonly misinterpreted in the West as meaning a negation and separation from family and friends, life and happiness—which, of course, is the opposite of what it actually means—that I have used a great many words to clarify the experiential, psychological, mental and emotional experience of attachments. I thought people needed to know this so that the logical reason why attachment should be eliminated would be obvious and logical based on everyone's personal experience. I also felt that the very detailed descriptions of the five states of Samadhi were also necessary so that the seeker of truth would know whether the result was worth all the trouble, with the hope that he or she would be inspired enough to believe that it is.

In fact, it is only after many years of writing and rewriting the Sutras, beginning with the briefest of translations—which I was never happy with because I knew that they would be virtually meaningless—that I finally decided to just say what the sutras mean no matter how many words were used. It was important to me that the book be understood in all its pragmatic advice.

For those of you who are interested in the original text, I have included a word-by-word Sanskrit to English transliteration and translation. I have also included a detailed Sanskrit glossary for every word in the Sutras, with listings for chapter and stanza numbers. The English index also covers most words and concepts that are contained in the original Sutras.

Although certainly your life can be vastly improved by reading and following the teachings of the Sutras on your own, I want to stress that a Realized Master, an Enlightened Guru, is absolutely necessary in addition to this book if you are to make any real or lasting progress. The mind is such a tricky magician that without the help of someone whose mirror is perfectly clear, you will be fooled.

It has been thrilling for me to write about the moment of creation, the Unified Field of the universe, Consciousness becoming the matter of the universe, the four levels of matter, the building blocks of nature— the triad of neutrons, protons and electrons, and, of course, the ascent of Consciousness back up through the levels of matter to Its own source. I especially love this book because it so perfectly describes, with great accuracy and perfect detail, my own Samadhi experiences; and so I know that what Master Patanjali has written is true. Luckily, with the new discoveries and theories in modern physics and cosmology, we at last have a few scientific terms in the English language to define the moment of the creation of the universe and the laws that govern it, written by the great Sage Patanjali some twenty five hundred years ago. Now, science must catch up to an understanding between Consciousness and the mind, and between the mind and the brain, which Master Patanjali has so eloquently written about.

Knowing how precious and valuable this book is has been my sole motivation for translating it. I pray that my work will in some small way benefit you, enable you to find happiness in everyday life, and attain the Supreme Happiness and Peace which comes through Self-Realization— which is the goal of life. May you be blessed.

Swami Savitripriya

Swami Savitripriya

Sunnyvale, California
April 24, 1991

❀

The Psychology of Mystical Awakening

The Patañjali Yoga Sutras

Chapter One

❀ Welcome! I greet you with folded hands and humbly bow before the Inner Light of your True-Self.

❀ *F*or those of you who desire to leave emotional suffering and unhappiness behind in favor of attaining a permanent state of peace and joy in daily life as the result of bringing your mind into harmonious oneness with the Eternal Consciousness of your True-Self, instruction will now begin on the scientific practices of the Psychology of Mystical Awakening. This self-directed psychology consists of physical, emotional and mental practices which enable you to break free from the limitation and suffering caused by identifying with the body, mind and ego; attain happiness in daily life; and ultimately reach the goal of Mystical Union: uniting your limited, individual consciousness and love with the Unlimited, Divine Consciousness and Love of your True-Self, and thus personally experience that it is the One Divine Consciousness which has become the world; because knowledge based on personal experience alone will make you free, not dogmas or belief systems. [1]

❀ *M*ystical Union with your True-Self is attained in stages as you cultivate the ability to voluntarily control the mental processes whereby you become able to prevent thought-waves from arising and disturbing the surface of the Lake of the Mind, which is composed of subtle physical matter, so that the mind becomes silent and the surface becomes calm. ₂

❀ *L*earning to keep the mind silent and tranquil is the necessary prerequisite for attaining Mystical Union with your all-pervading Conscious True-Self, for when no thoughts are arising from within the subtle Lake of the Mind, no neural firing can occur in the brain to produce brain wave patterns. Then, rather than Consciousness focusing on wave-images that appear on the surface of the Lake of the Mind, Consciousness remains established in, identified with, and exhibits Its own Eternal, Undiluted, Blissful Essence. [3]

But at all other times, when thought-waves are arising on the surface of the mind and producing neural firing in the brain, you, the Conscious-Seer within, become focused on, enmeshed in, and identified with, the wave-images, emotions and ideas that you see appearing on the surface of the mind. Thus, who a person believes him or herself to be is relative to the position Consciousness occupies: if the Center of Consciousness is positioned in the mind, Consciousness believes Itself to be the thoughts and emotions It has become one with; and if the Center of Consciousness is positioned within Itself, It sees the error of Its past beliefs, and discovers Its true identity. [4]

4

Chapter One

❀   *T*he first step in bringing order to the chaos that greets you as you first step back and become aware of the insanity and conflicts that are occurring in the mind is to become able to separate thoughts into five categories so you can identify which thoughts produce psychological suffering, and which ones do not, and instead, lead to a permanent state of peace. [5]

*T*he five categories of thoughts are:

Correct understanding

Incorrect understanding

Imagination

Deep dreamless sleep, and

Memory. [6]

Correct Understanding: You can only be certain that your understanding is correct if there is mutual agreement between three sources:

Your own direct personal perception;

The logical conclusion you reach based on inference; and

Receiving verification through examples in the scriptures or through the spoken words of an Enlightened Master. [7]

Incorrect Understanding: Incorrect understanding occurs when the Lake of the Mind is contaminated by one or more of the Five Causes of Suffering, for suffering causes the surface of the Lake of the Mind-Substance to be swept by stormy waves, rendering it incapable of clearly reflecting data and events

6

accurately, leading to your accumulating false knowledge which you believe to be true. [8]

Imagination: Imagination occurs when you, the Conscious-Seer, scan the recorded impressions in the mind-substance and embark on mental fantasy, linking together thoughts, emotions, ideas and words into scenarios that are void of all past and present knowledge based on personal experience of the external world. [9]

Deep Dreamless Sleep: Deep dreamless sleep occurs when Consciousness breaks the connection between Itself and the body/mind so that, since the Conscious-Seer is no longer focused on the impressions in the mind and providing the energy which enables thoughts to arise, no ideas and corresponding thought-waves arise to create the wave-images which produce dreams, and so only the brain-wave pattern characteristic of mental voidness is produced. [10]

Memory: When Consciousness focuses on previously recorded impressions and beliefs concerning actual personal experience of objects and events in the objective world which, right or wrong, are stored in the mind-field, it is called memory. [11]

7

❀   *T*he first thing you must do is form the habit of relinquishing highly charged emotional attachments to certain things, and aversions to others, in order to eliminate this basic cause of emotional suffering. You can recognize an attachment by becoming aware of every intense desire, expectation and demand that an object, person or event be responsible for your pleasure and happiness.

You can recognize an aversion by becoming aware of every intense fear that a particular sense object, person or event will cause you to experience the unhappiness you dread. Since immature deficiency demands keep the mind and emotions in a constant state of agitation, you must give up your dependency on others to make you happy.

This does not mean that you should give up friends and family, or not enjoy life, it only means that you should not become emotionally addicted so that you feel that you cannot survive or be happy without their approval, or their supplying your deficiency demands.

To eliminate attachments and aversions, you must learn to raise your Center of Consciousness up and out of the Lake of the Mind, remain poised in the place of the Director, and refuse to become emotionally devastated by any thought involving a desire or fear, by taking a slow, deep breath, and sincerely saying to yourself, 'I don't want to do this anymore. Let go.' This is the way to eliminate this cause of unnecessary suffering, and get off the emotional pendulum that swings between the opposites of desire and fear, love and hate, which create conflicting waves in the mind that collide with each other and create a stormy life experience. [12]

You must make a constant effort to observe and identify the nature of the different thoughts that arise in your mind; learn to remain detached and unaffected by them; and give up attitudes which cause strong emotional addictions whereby you greatly crave some things, while greatly fearing others. You must focus all of your attention exclusively on eliminating these basic causes of suffering, before attempting the next phase of the practice, because unless suffering caused by attachments and aversions is eliminated, the turbulence in your mind and emotions will prevent your further progress. [13]

Becoming firmly grounded in the position of refusing to live in a state of emotional devastation and suffering because others do not conform to your wishes will require total, unwavering commitment, without interruption or intervals, over a long period of time, because immature ego demands cannot be eliminated overnight. [14]

You will know when you have become free from attachments and aversions when you no longer thirst for emotional happiness from objects or events you have seen, experienced or heard about. [15]

❀   *O*nce you become free from emotional suffering caused by desires and fears, your mind and emotions will become calm. Then you will become aware of the permanent presence of Divine Consciousness and Love within your heart, which is so much more satisfying and complete than the best experiences of impermanent objects of the world composed of neutrons, protons and electrons that the question of thirsting for them no longer even arises. This is the highest state of non-attachment. [16]

*A*s your mind becomes more calm, you will reap the rewards of coming into direct contact with the limitless Ocean of Absolute Divine Truth, Consciousness and Bliss—your own True-Self—during the first four stages of Samadhi—Samprajnata Samadhi—the Samadhis which result in 'Enlightened Intelligence and Wisdom.' Samadhi is defined as an Expanded State of Consciousness that allows one to come face to face with Truths about the universe, God and man that can only be experienced when one's Consciousness temporarily transcends the limitations of the intellect, mind and senses.

The first stage of the Samadhi which results in Enlightened Intelligence and Wisdom—Vitarka Samadhi—the Samadhi of 'Active, Willful, Volitional Thinking', occurs through a focused awareness of the gross physical form of your object of meditation; and is accompanied by Consciousness becoming intimately connected with the object on the level of its gross physical form. As your focus becomes more steady, your Center of Consciousness penetrates deeper into the substratum of the object that underlies its outer physical form, and your awareness flows into the second stage.

The second stage of Samadhi—Vichara Samadhi— the Samadhi of 'Reflective Contemplation', is characterized by a lessening of thoughts and a more passive, though more powerfully centered, focus on the gross physical form of the object of meditation; and is accompanied by a joyous wonder as your Consciousness merges into, and becomes one with, the object on a deeper level of its gross physical form. As the thought process continues to lessen and the mind

becomes even more quiet, Consciousness effortlessly
expands into the third stage.

The third stage of Samadhi—Ananda Samadhi—the
Samadhi of 'Divine Bliss and Love', is characterized
by an even more passive, non-willful, non-volitional
focused awareness, however now, instead of an
awareness of the gross physical form of the object of
meditation, you find that you are floating in a vast
ocean of Conscious Love and Bliss, which is the
subtle, underlying support of the gross physical form
of the universe. This experience is accompanied by the
absolute conviction that you are an integral part of
this Eternal, Loving, Peaceful, Powerful Creative
Force. As the mental processes become even more
still, your Consciousness expands even farther until
you enter into the fourth stage of Samadhi and
become one with the heart of the universe.

The fourth stage of Samadhi—Asmita Samadhi—the Samadhi when one knows 'All of This is Me', is characterized by your complete lack of all volitional control and effort. Here you become aware that not only are you an integral part of this underlying benevolent energy that upholds the universe, but that you are It in Its entirety, and that everyone else and everything else is also this one Undivided Divine Conscious Self. During this Samadhi, you enter into oneness with the primal ocean of non-dual, Conscious Energy that has become the third dimension, and which has not yet divided Itself into separate, individual qualities and functions. This is accompanied by the experience of an indescribably vast, unfluctuating, Divine Peace, Power and Love.

Here, all questions are answered, all fear is removed, and you know that you will be satisfied forever. [17]

Chapter One

❀   S amprajnata Samadhi, the fifth and highest stage of Samadhi, which 'Transcends Enlightened Wisdom', follows. During this Samadhi, you, as Pure Consciousness, transcend the fourth stage of Samadhi and the Unified Field of the Universe and enter into the dimension of Eternity, which is the source of the Consciousness which has become the third dimensional world of nature. This Samadhi is entirely different from the previous four Samadhis because here, rather than Consciousness perceiving the different stages of Itself reflected on the surface of the mind-substance, Consciousness temporarily breaks Its connection with the mind and enters into Its own Undiluted, Unlimited, Ever-Unmanifested Wholeness, out of which came this minute speck of energy perceived as time, space and matter. Here, the degree and dimension of the pure Bliss, Love, Peace, Power, Intelligence, Benevolence and Goodness that was previously experienced during the fourth stage of Samadhi now increases to such a high degree that no words can describe the completeness of this most sublime experience. [18]

❀   *O*ccasionally, due to spiritual attainments in past lives, a rare soul spontaneously enters into the fourth stage of Samadhi, and
knows, 'All of This is Me', without having needed to
practice any spiritual disciplines in this life. His or her
Consciousness simply, without effort, merges into
oneness with the sum total of the basic matter of the
universe, called Prakriti, at which time even the
concept of being a separate, embodied individual
ceases to exist. [19]

But for all others, the fourth stage of the Samadhi when one knows 'All of This is Me' must be preceded by the development of The Four Foundations for Enlightenment:

> Faith in one's ability to succeed, the efficacy of the path, the ability of one's Master, and in the existence and benevolent support of the Divine Being;

> Heroic dedication to succeed in this extraordinary, and often times difficult, path to Self-Knowledge;

> Remembering the specific instructions of one's Master and the disciplines that must be practiced; and

> Progressing through the first three stages of the Samadhis which bring Enlightened Intelligence and Wisdom, which precede the fourth stage. [20]

❀ *I*f you are ardently enthusiastic in your practice, you will progress quickly and soon you, too, will become united with the Consciousness of the Universe during the fourth stage of Samadhi, and come to know, 'All of This is Me.' [21]

By increasing your efforts from mild to moderate, and from moderate to intense, you will find that your True-Self is also this special manifestation of Consciousness that has become the universe, and that your True-Self is essentially different from your mind and personality, and that it can be discovered by looking within. [22]

Personal effort is surely important, but the greatest source of progress is through a personal relationship with the personal facet of Absolute Divine Consciousness, called the Divine Being, which dwells within your heart. This is the Divine Being to whom you should surrender your mind and ego with faith and devotion, for in the end it is God's Grace alone which opens the door to Eternity, not the practices. [23]

Chapter One

❀   *T*he Divine Being is the personal aspect of Absolute Consciousness. The Divine Being, who is your True-Self, comes into manifestation as the third dimensional universe at the moment of creation, and creates, sustains and dissolves the universe in unending cycles. Although present in the midst of the universe of space, time and matter, the Divine Being is not subject to the karmic law of cause and effect, or bound by any third dimensional laws which govern the mortal body and mind which are composed of neutrons, protons and electrons. [24]

Since the Divine Being—who is your own True-Self—is the seed of All-Knowingness, It is not subject to ignorance and the suffering which ignorance produces. [25]

Unlimited by time and space, the Divine Being is also the Guru who, since the beginning, has appeared on earth in different bodies, taught humankind the truth, and then disappeared. [26]

In fact, the Divine Being is the Conscious Self of all creatures, for at the moment of each cycle of creation there issues forth the great sound-vibration OM as a minute particle of Consciousness smaller than the nucleus of an atom, and, containing everything that is to become the third dimensional universe, explodes forth from the Absolute dimension of the Spiritual Reality and becomes the universe of space, time and matter. Thus, since the sound OM—the sound of the instant of creation—originated from within the Divine Being, the sound of OM is also the Divine Being. [27]

❀   *T*hrough chanting OM, the sound of
the instant of creation, while listening
to its sound, bringing your Consciousness into its
vibration, and reflecting on its origin, an understanding of the reason that the background sound of OM
still reverberates throughout the universe, and an
understanding of the meaning and purpose of the
sound OM, will be born in your mind. [28]

From this inner awareness of the all-pervading
presence of Divine Consciousness, the darkness of
ignorance about who you are, and ignorance of the
origin, composition and purpose of the universe
which had previously pervaded your mind, will be
replaced by the Light of the knowledge that you are
all of this, which will prevent future obstacles caused
by ignorance of these facts, from coming into being. [29]

❀   *T*here are Nine Obstacles to Enlightenment, all of which are manifestations of the predominance of the inert, dark qualities associated with Tamas Guna, the neutronic force, which opposes movement, change and growth:

> *Physical illness:* the result of psychological disturbances caused by fear of change, growth, and the unknown which, through the sympathetic portion of the autonomic nervous system, causes imbalances in the functioning of the physical systems.

> *Resistance:* a rigid, stubborn, inflexible nature which resents correction, is determined to remain inflexible, and refuses to give up suffering in order to become happy.

> *Doubt:* regarding the promised results of the practices, one's own ability to succeed, and the ability of one's Master.

> *Disinterest:* a lack of enthusiasm, purpose and a higher goal.

> *Laziness:* physical and mental slothfulness and a tendency for self-indulgence.

Refusing to abstain from the prior bad habits that
have created pain and suffering; leading to
continued dependence on externals for
happiness.

Distorted vision of the Deity: leading to blaming
the Divine Being for the difficulties one
experiences in life; and expecting the Divine
Being to solve one's suffering rather than
making a personal effort.

Failure to make lasting gains: because of an
unwillingness to put forth the effort to practice the teachings that enable one to overcome
the obstacles, resulting in one's slipping back
so that one has to begin at the beginning each
time one decides to engage in the practices.

Mental unsteadiness: caused by fickle-
mindedness, scattered interest, and attention
on unimportant matters. [30]

*F*our Hindrances accompany the Nine Obstacles:

Psychological pain, suffering and unhappiness;

A bad disposition caused by anxiety and despair;

Lack of physical coordination; and

Uncontrolled breathing patterns marked by rapid, shallow irregular inhalations and exhalations. [31]

❀   *I*dentifying and then eliminating the suffering caused by the Nine Obstacles to Enlightenment constitutes the next level of the practice. This involves first identifying and naming the obstacles which are growing in your mindfield, and then counteracting them by the practice of planting and cultivating seeds of virtuous attitudes, thoughts and feelings that are the opposites of the obstacles. Then you must practice to form the habit of keeping your attention on feeling, cultivating, identifying with, and expressing the happiness and peace of the new virtuous attitudes rather than keeping your attention on the obstacles which cause suffering and trying to suppress them. Focusing your attention on the new positive qualities you are developing rather than on the negative ones you want to eliminate is the Yogic way of self-transformation. [32]

Chapter One

❀   *O*nce you have identified the obstacles in your mind, chosen the virtues you will replace them with, and are successfully feeling and expressing the new virtues in daily life, you may begin this next practice. This practice involves developing the habit of limiting your attitudes, thoughts, feelings and interactions with others solely to the following Four Virtuous Attitudes. You must practice these in relation to every object in the universe, sentient and insentient, composed of neutrons, protons and electrons, including yourself. You must carefully plant these seeds in your mind-field and cultivate them in order that your mind and emotions become clear, calm and happy. The Four Virtuous Attitudes you must cultivate are:

> *Friendliness* towards those who are happy;
>
> *Compassion* towards those who are suffering;
>
> *Rejoicing* towards those who are virtuous; and
>
> *Non-attached empathy* towards those whose actions are evil. [33]

❀ 　　*I*n addition, since there is an intimate connection between the breath and the mind, you should help your mind remain calm and silent by developing the habit of always breathing through your nose, and controlling your exhalation so as to make it as slow as your inhalation, thus making your breath slow and even. [34]

❀ *I*n order to bind your mind and keep it steady, you must lift your attention above unnecessary preoccupation with external objects composed of neutrons, protons and electrons, and above the multitude of distracting, inconsequential outer happenings that abound in daily life; $_{35}$

And instead, turn your attention back inwards and become one with the Effulgent Inner Light of your True-Self, which is beyond the sorrows that are experienced through the mind. $_{36}$

By keeping your attention focused on the Effulgent Inner Light of your True-Self instead of on random external sensory objects, your mind will cease to be excited and agitated due to desires that arise for objects composed of neutrons, protons and electrons, and thus will remain calm and peaceful. $_{37}$

Next, in order to eliminate the emotional suffering caused by unconscious motivations and reactions that arise from stored images that lie hidden deep within the Lake of the Mind and rule one's life from below surface Consciousness, you must analyze your dreams and gain an understanding of the natural connection between the information the dream is attempting to bring into Consciousness, and the impressions and images that are stamped upon the mind-substance which are the cause of the dream; and compare the mental, emotional and physical reactions that occur during the dream state with the mental, emotional and physical peace that is experienced during periods of deep dreamless sleep due to the absence of thought-waves and images; and gain an understanding of the natural connection between where Consciousness is focused in relation to these two states of mind. [38]

❀   *F*or the more formal aspects of the
practice, choose the name and form of
the Divine Being that you hold most dear, which you
will consistently use as the single object you will focus
your attention on each time you sit to practice
meditation. [39]

Eventually, through consistently focusing your mind
on this one single object, thoughts will diminish and
then, during the four states of Samadhi, you will come
to know the inner subtle physical essence of this
object, and of all other objects in the universe as well,
from the most minute form of subtle energy to the
totality of the expanding cosmos. After this, you will
not be bound by the universe, and instead the universe will be subject to your Enlightened Will. [40]

By using only one object to focus your attention on
during the practice of meditation, the wave-images in
your mind will become so weak that they will almost
stop. Then the Lake of the Mind-Substance will
become 'clear', 'colorless' and 'transparent' like a
crystal, and so perfectly reflect the reality that 'the one
who is knowing', 'the act of knowing', and 'the object

Chapter One

known', are one and the same. Since the Lake of the Mind becomes totally permeated by this one single reflection, it becomes identical with it in the same way that a crystal becomes the color of the object it reflects. This describes the non-dual fourth stage of Samadhi. [41]

But during the first stage of Samadhi—Savitarka Samadhi—the Samadhi of 'Active, Volitional, Willful Thinking', which is characterized by the act of mental examination of the gross physical form of the object of meditation, you experience duality between yourself, the Conscious-Seer who is the subject, and the gross physical form of the object of meditation. During this first stage of Samadhi, you are aware of the sound of the word that designates this object; the object which is connected with the word; personal knowledge you have gained in relation to the object; and imagination concerning the object. Thus, during the first stage of Samadhi, one's focus rapidly fluctuates between these four types of thought-waves concerning the gross physical form of the object of meditation. [42]

Next, during the second stage of Samadhi—Nirvitarka Samadhi—the Samadhi of 'Ceasing to Willfully and Logically Examine the Object of Meditation', the Lake of the Mind-Substance becomes more calm, for thought-waves that would ordinarily arise from memory and differentiate between the sound of the name of the object, the object which is connected with the word, personal knowledge about the object, and imagination concerning it, now no longer arise. Thus, since memory-thoughts have ceased, the duality which you previously imagined to exist between yourself, the Conscious Subject, and the object you are perceiving disappears, and so the calm Lake of the Mind now only reflects the gross physical object of meditation. Thus, at this stage of Samadhi, the illusion of duality is replaced by the profound experience of Consciousness merging into oneness with the gross physical form of your object of meditation. [43]

During the third stage of Samadhi-Savichara Samadhi-the Samadhi of 'Reflective Contemplation', the thought process slows down even more and, although duality is once again experienced between yourself, the Conscious subject, and your object of meditation, the ever-increasing stillness of your mind allows you, Consciousness, to enter into, and perceive, the sub atomic level of matter, of which the gross physical characteristics of the object are composed.

Next, during the fourth stage of Samadhi-Nirvichara Samadhi-the Samadhi of 'Ceasing to Reflectively Contemplate the Object', the thought process almost ceases altogether, leaving Consciousness to the totality of Itself, at the level of the Ocean of Primal, Undifferentiated Energy. At this time, all duality between yourself as the Conscious subject, and the object, which is now the totality of the undifferentiated energy which upholds the universe, disappears. This is the highest and most complete experience of the underlying, non-dual substance of the universe, when you know, 'All of This is Me'.

The third and fourth stages of Samadhi can be distinguished from each other in the same way that the first and second stages are distinguished from each other. That is, in the first stage of Samadhi, duality is experienced between yourself, the Conscious subject, and the form of your object of meditation; while in the second stage you, the Conscious subject, and your object of meditation, become one. In the same way, in the third stage of Samadhi, duality is again experienced between yourself, the Conscious subject, and the object of meditation; while in the fourth stage you experience the state of non-duality.

The difference between the first and second stage, and the third and fourth stage, is that in the first and second stages, you are aware of the gross physical level of the object of meditation; while in the third and fourth stages you are aware of the sum total of the subtle, sub atomic levels of energy which composes the Ocean of Energy/Matter which is the underlying subtle basis of all gross physical forms. [44]

When, during the fourth stage of Samadhi, one's Consciousness merges into perfect, non-dual union with Itself at the level of the Unified Field of the Universe, which constitutes the very fabric of nature—the undifferentiated matter out of which are born the neutrons, protons and electrons which compose the objects of the senses—and knows 'All of This is Me', one has reached the far limits of the subtle energy-matter of the universe beyond the experiences which produce impressions that result in rebirth. [45]

Here, only the one wave-image of the single experience, 'All of this seed matter of the universe is me', washes over the mind-substance and leaves a seed impression of this experience, which is observed as a reflection on the surface of the mind. [46]

This single wave-impression that flows through the mind during this fourth stage of the Samadhi that Transcends Reflective Contemplation purifies the mind to such a degree that the mind-substance becomes perfectly clear, and so now perfectly reflects the wholeness of the universe which, through the mind and senses, appears to consist of separate and completely individual parts. [47]

Once, through this realization, the mind-substance is purified of distorting impressions, it clearly reflects the Divine Physical Laws which control the universe, and thus this mind, which is now Enlightened with a New Intelligence and Wisdom, is called The Bearer of Truth. [48]

While ordinary minds bear knowledge of third dimensional objects composed of neutrons, protons and electrons that is based on hearsay, or based on intellectual conclusions drawn from sensory impressions, the mind which has become the Bearer of Truth is totally different. This enlightened mind understands the Divine origin and underlying purpose of the universe composed of neutrons, protons and electrons, for this special mind, now functioning from a new enlightened intelligence and wisdom, sees into the underlying essence of all objects. [49]

❀ *O*ne's mind can only become free of
distorted concepts and personal
biases, based on incorrect knowledge which clouds
one's perception and understanding, after one has
experienced the fourth stage of Samadhi, for the
wave impression born of that experience obstructs
past impressions obtained through the limitations of
the mind and senses, and prevents them from inter-
fering with the direct perception of Truth. [50]

❀   When, during the fourth stage of Samadhi, all thought-waves completely cease, you will enter into the fifth stage of Samadhi—Asamprajnata Samadhi—the 'Samadhi Which Transcends the Four States of Samadhi Which Bring Enlightened Intelligence and Wisdom.' During this fifth stage of Samadhi, you will merge into oneness with the totality of Pure, Undiluted Consciousness, and transcend the third dimension altogether. At this time you enter into the Indescribable Eternity of the seventh dimension—the dimension of Absolute Consciousness, the dimension of the Absolute Spiritual Reality. Now Consciousness is completely separated from the seed matter of the universe, and completely separated from the mind, and so no thought process occurs. Thus, only this fifth stage of Samadhi is called 'seedless'. Now there remains no possibility that a latent seed impression could, in the future, propel you back into rebirth to fulfill a forgotten desire. [51]

Chapter Two

❀   *T*he next level of the practice involves
developing and balancing your will,
intellect and heart through developing Three Self-
Directed Strengths, upon which the success of the
remainder of the practice of the Psychology of Mystical Awakening rests:

> *Self-directed discipline:* whereby your will
> becomes strengthened as you refuse to give in
> to ignorant attitudes, thoughts and emotions
> which are obstacles to happiness and to
> expanded states of Consciousness. This
> discipline necessitates a willingness to endure
> the psychological suffering of the ego that
> may at times accompany truth and change;
> and the Conscious decision to let go of all
> preconceived ideas about yourself in order to
> grow and become mature, self-sufficient and
> happy.

Self-directed meditation and analysis of *your thoughts and feelings:* whereby your intellect becomes strengthened as you actively become the Director of your mind in order to constantly monitor and direct your thoughts and feelings. This discipline necessitates the willingness to own every thought and feeling, especially those which you have previously tried to hide from, because everything that you refuse to accept as existing within you will continue to grow ever larger, and influence your life from below surface Consciousness. Therefore, you must decide to become aware of every unpleasant thought and feeling, and compassionately and deeply understand and educate these ignorant, immature parts of yourself as if they were your younger brothers or sisters. Then the energies that were bound up in conflicts will be released to assist you in your efforts, instead of their working against you.

Self-directed surrender, love and devotion to the Divine Being who is your True-Self: in order to open your heart by surrendering your mind and ego to the Divine Being within. As you develop trust and humility before a power greater than your ego-self, the lotus of your heart will open, and the power of love will support your quest. [1]

❀   *T*he purpose of actively strengthening and balancing your will, intellect and heart is that the power you gain through developing and balancing each of these parts of yourself will enable you to take the necessary steps to reduce the Five Causes of Suffering so that you will be able to discover your own All-Pervading, Blissful, True-Self during the states of Samadhi. $_2$

❀   *T*he Five Causes of Suffering are linked
       together in a cause and effect sequence:

The basis of suffering is ignorance. To be
ignorant is to be oblivious of the origin and
composition of the universe, and of the inner
presence of the Eternal, Blissful and Conscious
True-Self. This leads to the belief:

'I am my body, emotions, mind and intellect',
which results in;

A constant state of mental, emotional and
physical agitation due to a desire to obtain
pleasure and happiness through external
objects which stimulate the senses and bring
the physical and emotional pleasure, which
results in;

A state of constant mental, emotional and physical agitation due to an aversion and fear that objects or events will not fulfill one's desires, and thus cause one to feel unhappy, which results in;

A tenacious determination to continue trying to obtain an unbroken experience of physical pleasure and emotional happiness through obtaining the objects of sensory pleasure which one desires, and avoiding those which one fears, even though experience proves that lasting pleasure and happiness is not experienced through a life focused on fulfilling the unending desires of the senses. [3]

❀ *I*gnorance of the fact that the Eternal Peace, Love and Happiness that one is seeking outside is already within one's own True-Self, and instead believing that one is the mortal body, mind and personality, creates the conditions in the mind-field for the seeds of the other four causes of suffering to grow. Although ignorance, and the resulting beliefs, are present in all minds which have not yet become purified during the fourth stage of Samadhi, the control they have over the mind and emotions varies according to their intensity. For example, ignorant beliefs and their results are:

> *Exceedingly strong and active* in the average person who does not understand, or care to believe, that he or she is not the mind, emotions or body; that his or her view of the third dimensional universe is less than accurate; and thus does nothing to counteract the causes of suffering;

47

Are becoming reduced in a person who is actively engaged in the practices of this psychology and is cultivating the Three Self-Strengthening Supports;

Have become weak in a person who is in an advanced stage of the practice, and who can now easily intercept them during their infrequent appearance; and

Have become dormant in a person who has reduced them to a seed state. ₄

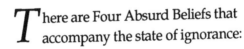

*T*here are Four Absurd Beliefs that accompany the state of ignorance:

The belief that people and objects, all of which are composed of neutrons, protons and electrons, and which are in a constant state of transformation and change, will remain the same and will not change or disappear;

The belief that the body, which is only a machine which produces waste products; and the mind, which ordinarily contains mostly misconceptions, are pure;

The belief that the high degree of emotional pain and suffering which most people experience throughout life is the state of happiness; and

The belief that the body is humankind's spiritual essence and thus should be worshipped, when actually the body, and the impressions in the mind which constitute the personality, are only inert objects composed of neutrons, protons and electrons. [5]

The first cause of ignorance, the belief, 'This body and mind is who I am', occurs when the Conscious Seer projects Its power down into Its unconscious body and mind, and then believes that these two things—Consciousness, and the body/mind—are essentially the same, and thus that the mind is Conscious. 6

This leads to the desire to obtain physical and emotional pleasure through external sensory objects, in order to experience pleasure and happiness, which leads to highly charged mental and emotional states of suffering rather than to the happiness one desires. 7

This leads to aversions and fear that particular persons, objects, or events might think, say or do something that might cause you to feel the dreaded state of unhappiness, which, of course, produces the feared result. 8

This leads to a tenacious determination to, at all costs, continue repeating the same patterns of attempting to feel continual pleasure and happiness through having one's immature deficiency demands fulfilled through external sensory objects composed of neutrons, protons and electrons. This driving desire for pleasure is deeply rooted in the creatures of the earth, and arises from remembered experiences connected with the primitive drives that exist in the lower forms of life through which one has evolved, and which one remembers and still acts upon. This consuming desire for pleasure flows with a strong current of its own, causing one to often times become engaged in degrading actions when actually one is seeking the lost Bliss and Love which lies hidden within one's own heart. [9]

❀   *I*n order to eliminate these Five Causes
of Suffering, you must weaken them
and then reduce them to a subtle, inactive state
through constantly rejecting the ideas they produce.
This is accomplished in daily life through keeping
your Center of Consciousness above the Lake of the
Mind and actively being the Director so you can, first,
refrain from acting on any impulses that arise from
any of the causes of suffering, and secondly, refuse to
accept that ignorant thoughts are true. Next, reverse
the energy of the thought, and follow it down to the
seed impression out of which it arose, and compassionately educate that ignorant, immature, primitive
part of yourself by compassionately explaining to it
the truth, and then bringing it into your own more
mature level of understanding. In this way, inner
conflict will be avoided as you integrate your mind
and personality around a higher Center of Consciousness. [10]

❀ *E*ven after you have reduced the Five Causes of Suffering to subtle seed states so that they are no longer active in daily life, they may still at times produce memory thought-waves when you begin to practice meditation. If this happens, you must continue to refuse to accept as truth any ideas associated with the Five Causes of Suffering. 11

Because even if you eliminate their outer manifestation each time they arise, as long as their roots have not been pulled out of the mind-field—which is the storehouse of karma—they will continue to sprout and produce suffering, both in this life and in lives still to come. 12

Any cause of suffering that remains rooted in the mind-field will cause you to be reborn again into a particular species, circumstances, life span, and experiences of pleasure and pain which correspond to their stored impressions, in order that you may fulfill all unfulfilled desires. [13]

When the five root causes of suffering produce fruit of good and virtuous karma, you will have experiences that are refreshing, pleasurable and delightful; and when the causes of suffering produce fruit of bad and evil karma, you will have experiences that are hot, tormenting and difficult. [14]

❀   *B*ut when you analyze both the imme-
diate and the future results of the
inborn desire for pleasure, and discriminate between
pleasant and painful emotions, you will see that
obtaining experiences of pleasure that are based on
the Five Causes of Suffering result in pain rather than
in the anticipated pleasure. This occurs because a
tormenting fear of change and future loss is inherent
in the experience of pleasure; and, since each experience of pleasure strengthens the mental impressions
that cause one to seek to repeat the experience, one
remains in a state of fear and anxiety that the object of
desire will not be available in the future; which causes
one to direct all of one's energy on seeking to obtain it;
and then, when finally getting it, again increasing the
strength of the attachment to this object which impels
one to repeat the experience yet again; and on ad
infinitum as the impression continues to gain
strength. These conflicting mind-waves that oscillate
between experiences of pleasure and pain are the
cause of great suffering. [15]

❀ *P*ain and suffering that have not yet
begin to flow can be avoided. [16]

Since suffering can only occur if you, the Conscious Seer, are focused on, and identifying with, the wave images and emotions which you see appearing on the surface of the mind, you can avoid future suffering by resisting the impulse to become one with, and act out, desires and fears that produce suffering. [17]

❀   *P*lease remember this important fact: everything in the universe—sentient and insentient—objects, people, plants, animals, the mind-substance, everything—is composed of different combinations of the three sub atomic particles, and the three qualities which they represent: electrons, which represent illuminative understanding, balance and happiness; protons, which represent passionate excitement, movement and suffering; and neutrons, which represent dark ignorance, stillness and dullness. These three build-ing blocks of nature then gather together in different combinations to form the five natural elements: ether, air, fire, water and earth; which in turn compose the physical matter of the universe, from the subtle mind-substance which carries te recorded events of each life and is a part of thesubtle body that accompanies the soul from birth to birth , to

57

the most gross level of physical objects, such as rocks. All third dimensional experience takes place through the interaction of the senses with sensory objects, both of which are composed of neutrons, protons and electrons. The purpose of the universe is to provide the Conscious Seer with sensory experiences so that by analyzing the results of both pleasure and pain, you, the Conscious Seer, will eventually discover that you are eternal, and that you are not your body and mind. Thus, through discriminating between your own Consciousness and your body and mind, you discover that Divine Love and Bliss is within your True-Self, and become free from being bound to matter. This is the purpose of the world. [18]

❀   *T*here are four distinct levels of the development and evolution of Consciousness/matter as it evolves from the first level of the Unified Field to the level of neutrons, protons and electrons that form the building blocks of the world:

> *The first level* of the descent of Consciousness
> becoming matter occurs at the beginning of
> time, at the moment of creation when Divine
> Consciousness explodes the minute, highly
> condensed, particle of Itself that is to become
> the sum total of the universe of space, time
> and matter forth from the totality of Its Abso-
> lute Eternal Dimension—the Divine Spiritual
> Dimension—into the expanding, Unified
> Field of Consciousness/Matter—complete, in
> perfect balance, and as yet undivided into
> separate laws, qualities or attributes—yet
> containing within Itself all of the potential
> forms of the universe.

The second level occurs a billionth of a second later when, as the hot, expanding Unified Field of Consciousness/Matter begins to cool, a disequilibrium occurs, and the Unified Field divides Itself into the first subtle attributes and forms of separate energy forces, functions, and laws that will govern and build the third dimensional world of nature.

The third level occurs as the forces of the universe evolve into more specialized laws that will govern mind and matter, and into the more specialized forms—the neutrons, protons and electrons—that will be the building blocks of nature.

The fourth and most gross level occurs as the sub atomic forces gather together into complex units and become the spinning, pulsating, atoms and molecules which, then, appear to the mind and senses to be solid, gross, physical objects. [19]

❀   *T*he Consciousness of the Embodied
Seer always remains absolutely pure,
but when the Seer is perceiving the universe through
the instrument of the mind, the underlying essence of
the universe is hidden beneath the wave-images of
the thought process. [20]

This is why when viewed through the mind and
senses, the Conscious True-Self believes the universe
to be the waves which ripple across the surface of the
Lake of the Mind. [21]

Thus, the purpose of life can only be fulfilled when
you retrace the descent of Consciousness back
through the gross levels of matter to Its origin until,
for you, the gross physical form of the universe
dissolves into the undivided unified field; although its
physical form continues to exist for all others who are
concentrated on the gross physical level of matter, and
continues to provide common experiences. [22]

It is only when you, the Owner and Master of the Body and Mind, project your Power and Light of Consciousness down into the instrument you occupy, and enter into oneness with it, that you believe you are the contents of your mind. [23]

This impulse to identify with the body and mind is the cause of ignorance. [24]

When the impulse to identify with your body and mind disappears, ignorance also disappears enabling you, the Conscious Seer, to become separated from your identification with matter. [25]

❀ *T*he means to remove this impulse is unwavering, assertive analysis of the difference between yourself—the Conscious Seer—and your body and mind. [26]

❀   N ext, as you become firmly grounded in the following seven steps of the practice, you must continue to unceasingly analyze the difference between yourself as Consciousness, and your body and mind. This will enable you to reach Samadhi, the eighth and last step of the practice, which will result in a new, Higher Intelligence and Wisdom. [27]

But in order to attain the state of mind that will enable you to experience the Divine Truth/Consciousness/Blissful Love that is experienced during the states of Samadhi, you must first successfully carry out the instructions of the preceding seven steps of the practice while continuing to assertively analyze the difference between yourself, Consciousness, and the mental processes that you observe in your mind. As a result of this discrimination, mental impurities will diminish as your mind become filled with the Light of Knowledge due to your direct experience of the truth about yourself, the universe and God that lies hidden within all of the forms of the world. [28]

While all of the practices up to this point have been disciplines which eliminate psychological and emotional suffering, and purify the mind in preparation for these next more advanced practices of Yoga Psychology, these last eight practices which I will teach you constitute the actual methods which are the means that will enable you to retrace the descent of Consciousness back to Its first level of manifestation as the Primal Ocean of the unified field. The following are the last eight steps of the practice:

❀ Become the embodiment of the Five Virtues for Happy Relationships.

❀ Become the embodiment of the Five Virtues for Happy Personal Life.

❀ Develop the Happy Sitting Posture for Meditation.

❀ Become proficient in Breathing Patterns to relax the body and silence the mind.

❀ Develop the ability to Turn Your Senses Inwards and voluntarily break their connection with externals.

❀ Become proficient in Concentrating your mind on the single object of your choice.

❀ Become proficient in Meditating on the single object of your choice.

❀ Spontaneously enter into the super-conscious states of Samadhi and discover your True Eternal-Self.[29]

❀ The Five Virtues for Happy Relationships must become the basis of all of your interactions with every part of the universe, for these virtues will promote harmony with society, minimize disturbances in mind and body, and lead to increased peace and happiness:

> Do not be violent, angry or aggressive towards others.
>
> Do not lie to others.
>
> Do not steal from others.
>
> Do not lust over others.
>
> Do not be selfish towards others. [30]

These Five Virtues for Happy Relationships must apply to every facet of your life, without exception, irrespective of species, time, location, or circumstances. Vowing to always feel and express these five virtues, and to never relate to any level of the universe in ways that are contrary to them, is the greatest vow that anyone can ever take. [31]

❀ Secondly are the Five Virtues for Happy Personal Life, which must be the basis of your existence, for these virtues will also promote harmony within society, minimize disturbances in mind and body, and lead to increased peace and happiness:

> Remain clean and undefiled in body, mind and environment.
>
> Remain content to fulfill your personal Dharma.
>
> Remain self-disciplined and resist ignorant thoughts and behavior.
>
> Remain in control of your mind, and study your thoughts, feelings, words and actions. And,
>
> Remain mentally and emotionally surrendered to, and focused on, the Divine Being within you—who is your True-Self—with ever increasing faith, love and devotion. [32]

❀　Whenever a non-virtuous thought or feeling arises that is contrary to these Ten Virtues for Happiness, whether it is about yourself, your life, or about others, you must first recognize it, own it, and admit that this thought is a part of who you are on the level of your third dimensional personality. Next, you must replace the non-virtuous thought and feeling with a virtuous one that is the opposite of the one that was negative, and feel the virtue filling your very being, until you actually become the embodiment of this virtue: intellectually, emotionally, and within every cell of your body. [33]

Every violent thought, word or deed—such as the violence of aggression, lying, stealing, lust, selfishness and so on—whether it is directed toward yourself or another; whether you commit the deed yourself, cause another to do it, or approve of it being done; whether it has arisen from greed, anger or delusion; or whether it is expressed in a mild, moderate or intense degree; always results in an endless cycle of suffering and unhappiness, and stands in the way of your gaining personal knowledge and truth.

Therefore, to break the cycle of suffering, you must plant and cultivate the seeds of the Ten Virtues for Happiness within yourself that are the opposites of the non-virtuous ones, and thereby put an end to your violent behavior. By doing this, you will reap untold personal rewards. I will tell you of the benefits; first for the Five Virtues for Happy Relationships: [34]

When you plant the seed of compassionate understanding within yourself, which is the opposite of violence, anger and aggression, and cultivate it by practicing feeling it sprout and grow within you so that you actually become the embodiment of compassionate understanding—intellectually, emotionally and within every cell of your body—you will no longer think, feel or act violent, angry or aggressive even if you find yourself in the midst of their presence; [35]

When you plant the seed of truthfulness within yourself, which is the opposite of lying and deceit, and cultivate it by practicing feeling it sprout and grow within you so that you actually become the embodiment of truthfulness—intellectually, emotionally and within every cell of your body—truth will then be the deciding factor upon which you base all of your actions, whatever the consequences may be; 36

When you plant the seed of honesty within yourself, which is the opposite of stealing, and cultivate it by practicing feeling it sprout and grow within you so that you actually become the embodiment of honesty—intellectually, emotionally and within every cell of your body—wealth equal to the rarest jewels will come and abide with you, and supply your every need; 37

When you plant the seed of loving chastity within yourself, which is the opposite of passionate lust, and cultivate it by practicing feeling it sprout and grow within you so that you actually become the embodiment of loving chastity—intellectually, emotionally and within every cell of your body—you will gain the strength and the qualities that are associated with a shining hero; 38

71

When you plant the seed of self-sufficiency within yourself, and become disinterested in amassing possessions or accepting gifts that have strings attached, which is the opposite of being dependent and selfishly collecting and hoarding objects, and cultivate these by practicing feeling them sprout and grow within you so that you actually become the embodiment of self-sufficiency and disinterest in amassing possessions—intellectually, emotionally and within every cell of your body—you will gain a perfect understanding of the how and why of this birth, which will answer all of your questions about your life. [39]

❀   N ext, by planting the seeds of the Five Virtues of Happy Personal Life within yourself, cultivating them within yourself in the same way you cultivated and grew the Five Virtues of Happy Relationships, you will gain an equal degree of increased happiness.

Thus, by becoming the actual embodiment of purity—intellectually, emotionally and within every cell of your body—you will become indifferent to the various parts of your own body, and will choose to remain distant and free from coming into contact with the bodies of others. [40]

Then, since your mind will be focused one-pointedly on the practices due to victory over your senses, it will remain cheerful and filled with light, joy and peace. Once your mind has attained this degree of purity, you will be capable of Mystical Union, and will have the direct vision that you and the Deity are one. [41]

By becoming the actual embodiment of contentment, graciously and willingly accepting every experience life places before you, while striving to learn and improve yourself through it, knowing that every thing that happens is the perfect thing through which you can gain greater understanding and maturity, you will attain a state of continual happiness that cannot be excelled; $_{42}$

By becoming the actual embodiment of the willingness to undergo any psychological suffering of the ego in regards to changing negative, unvirtuous thoughts and impulses in order that you may attain a state of peaceful enlightenment; and the willingness to welcome the purifying heat that results from this self-imposed austerity whereby you burn up the seeds of suffering by offering them into the Fire of Knowledge, you will become perfect in body, mind and senses; $_{43}$

By becoming the actual embodiment of self-study, whereby you constantly monitor your thoughts and reverse those that are impure in order to locate their source and transform this energy into the virtues, you will become the embodiment of the qualities expressed by the form of the Deity you most love, and will become united with your chosen form of the Deity in heart and mind; $_{44}$

By becoming the actual embodiment of ever-increasing surrender of your mind and egoistic thoughts and attitudes to the Divine Being within you, you will attain the states of Samadhi through Grace, and then your Consciousness will remain in a permanent state of perfect Love. [45]

✿ *A*fter you have cultivated and grown the Ten Virtues for Happiness within yourself, you may devote yourself to this next practice. This involves developing the Happy Sitting Posture for Meditation: sitting on a comfortable but firm surface, legs crossed, knees touching the floor, and spine and neck in a straight line. Little by little your leg muscles will become loose, your back and neck muscles strong, and your body steady, so that soon it will be easy and comfortable for you to happily sit in this posture for long periods of time. [46]

As your body becomes stronger and more relaxed, and less effort is required to maintain it in the proper meditation posture, your mind will also become more relaxed. Then there are times when you will feel as if your body and mind dissolve, and that you are merging into oneness with endless space. [47]

When your mind becomes this still, you will not be disturbed by the pairs of opposites such as desire and fear that arise from impressions based on ignorance. [48]

❀ Once you are able to sit happily in the meditation posture, you must learn to regulate the inward and outward flow of breath, and the duration between each breath, in a certain prescribed manner that will further calm your mind, and purify the subtle nerve channels in your body. 49

These specific breathing patterns determine whether the inhalations and exhalations are full and slow or partial and fast; whether the emphasis is on pulling the breath in or pushing it out; the number of seconds used during each process; and the number of rounds practiced. These breathing exercises have such a beneficial and quieting effect on the body and mind that often times the Lake of the Mind becomes absolutely still as thoughts completely stop. 50

When this occurs, Consciousness transcends awareness of the breathing process, transcends the gross physical level of the universe of forms which is normally perceived by the mind and senses, and enters into the exalted fourth stage of Samadhi, which I previously explained and described. 51

At this moment, the veil of the mind composed of neutrons, protons and electrons, which previously hid the Light of your True-Self, dissolves, revealing your own Effulgent Consciousness. [52]

Concentrating on the breath is the method which will quiet your mind, and prepare you for the direct vision of the Light of your own True-Self. [53]

❀ The next level of the practice is becoming proficient in Turning the Senses Inward in order to temporarily sever the link between your mind and senses, and external stimuli. This will enable you to become aware of, analyze, and resolve the unconscious contents of your mind so that no thought or feeling remains hidden from you. Thus, after concentrating the mind on the breath to quiet the thought process, you must practice turning your senses back inwards and dissolve them into the mind-substance, thereby breaking the link between the senses and the external world. Then, since your mind will have become stilled by the breathing processes, you will not be disturbed by random memory thoughts of the past; or current thoughts of the present; and since you have broken the link between the mind and senses and external stimuli, you will not be disturbed by incoming sensory data. This enables you to separate and disentangle yourself from the

conflicts and contradictions that are occurring in the mental field so that you can look down into the Lake of the Mind and become aware of thoughts and feelings that you are not normally aware of. Remaining above the surface of the mind, observe the stream of thoughts, feelings, images and fantasies that arise like bubbles from the dark depths of the Lake of the Mind. Without becoming mentally or emotionally involved, listen to the sentences, feel the feelings, and accept the fact that these often unwanted parts of yourself do actually exist. Then, reversing their energy, follow them down into their source, understand the cause, and then educate them. This is the way to release tensions and clear your mind-substance of unconscious or unresolved causes of suffering which, if you do not bring into your awareness and resolve, will continually distract you when you try to meditate, and will also influence your daily life negatively, often from below the surface of awareness. [54]

80

❀ *A*fter you have purified your mind in this manner, and brought all of the previously unconscious impressions up from the unconscious and into the Light of awareness, the Lake of the Mind will be clear and transparent, enabling you, the Conscious Seer, to be the unchallenged master of your mind instead of being the slave to the suffering caused by past impressions that were born of ignorance. [55]

81

Chapter Three

❀   Concentration, the sixth step, may be practiced after you have brought the more gross levels of your being—behavior, body, Pranic life energy and senses—under control; and after you have brought all hidden mental impressions up and into the Light of Consciousness and transformed them during the practice of Drawing the Senses Inward. Now, the practice of Concentration will allow you to gain more direct control over your thoughts. Concentration is defined as binding the sum-total of the mind-substance to one single physical object, pulling your attention back again and again to the gross physical form of your object each time it wanders. In the beginning you may concentrate upon the object of meditation with your eyes open. Soon you will be able to close your eyes and easily visualize its form in your mind. [1]

❀ Meditation, the seventh step, is defined as an advanced stage of Concentration when there has become less struggle to keep your attention focused solely on the single object. Meditation is attained when extraneous thoughts cease, and only the one wave-image of your object flows across the Lake of the Mind. [2]

❀   Samadhi, the eighth and last step of the practice, is an advanced stage of Meditation, and is experienced during five progressively higher stages of Expanded Consciousness. During the states of Samadhi, one experiences transcendental levels of Truth beyond that which can be known through the intellect, mind and senses. While during the first stage of Samadhi you are aware of the gross physical level of form of the object of meditation, during the fourth stage of Samadhi, the gross physical level of the object dissolves as you penetrate deeper into the atomic substratum of the object. At this level of awareness, you transcend the single object as your consciousness expands into oneness with the sum total of the most subtle level of matter that upholds all gross physical forms; until during the fifth stage of Samadhi, your Consciousness transcends the subtle physical matter of the third dimension completely, during which time your mind is completely void of thoughts. ₃

85

�֎   *T*hese three practices—Concentration,
Meditation and Samadhi—when
practiced together in sequence, one after the other—
are called the practice of Becoming the Object. This
threefold practice enables you to enter into the underlying subtle field of matter which composes the object
you are observing in order to enter into non-dual
oneness with it, because the only way to truly know
an object is to become the object. This is the aim of this
psychology₄

❀   *A*s you master this threefold practice, and become united in non-dual oneness with the sum total of the Divine Consciousness and Love which has become the form of the world, a new Enlightened Intelligence and Wisdom—which can only be attained through a direct personal experience of Transcendental Truth—will illumine your mind, and destroy the darkness of ignorance. 5

Chapter Three

❀   The ability to Become the Object of the universe is attained in stages. First, during the practice of Concentration, you gain the ability to focus your attention by pulling your mind back again and again to the object each time it wanders. Then, during the practice of Meditation, you continue to perfect your ability to focus your attention on one object until only the wave-image of that object repeatedly flows through your mind. Next, your Consciousness begins to transcend the mind and senses as It expands into Samadhi, which begins with the gross physical level of one form filling your mind, and ends with your Consciousness becoming one with the sum total of the conscious energy which composes the Unified Field of the Universe.

This is an intellectual explanation of the ascent of Consciousness through matter to Its most rarefied third dimensional state, at the very edge of the third dimensional universe of space, time and matter.

The personal aesthetic experience of the ascent of Consciousness from Its manifestation as matter to Its original Infinite, undiluted state is the experience of becoming one with Infinite Divine Love, Bliss, Peace and Knowledge which is an experience so great that it is beyond description.[6]

❀   When compared with the five preceding practices, which were preparatory steps concerned with externals such as developing the Virtues for Happy Relationships and Personal Life, becoming able to maintain the Happy Sitting Posture for Meditation, developing Proper Breathing Patterns, and becoming adept in the practice of Withdrawing the Senses Inward— all in order to clear and purify the mind-substance—the three practices of Concentration, Meditation and Samadhi are considered to be internal.₇

But when these three practices are compared with the fifth 'Seedless' stage of Samadhi —when Consciousness transcends the seeds of matter that are known during the fourth stage—and becomes the totality of the Seventh, Infinite, Spiritual Dimension within which this minute third dimensional universe exists, they, too, are considered to be external. ₈

This can be understood by the following examples:

During the practice of Concentration on the gross physical form of your object, the mind-substance undergoes constant transformation: each time a thought-wave arises as the result of your mind pursuing an outer event, a thought-wave arises which you must suppress and dissolve; each time a thought arises from a stored impression, you must overpower it; each time you see a visual image, you must dissolve it back into its source. Thus, a transformation occurs in the mind-substance each time you suppress and dissolve a thought, and sever the cause and effect link between Consciousness and the impression out of which the thought arose. These transformations occur within a succession of space-time frames that represent the smallest degree of change that can occur in matter, corresponding to the fastest movement of sub atomic particles from one point in space to another; and which occur within the smallest measurement of time, beyond which no further division can take place. Each of the space-time frames indicates the most minute degree of the decay and transformation of matter on the sub atomic level. [9]

Next, during the practice of Meditation, the suppressing impression becomes larger and more powerful until only the suppressing wave arises from its seed impression and repeatedly flows through the mind-substance. Thus, during the practice of meditation, the mind-substance becomes transformed by the one wave which suppresses other thoughts and prevents them from arising. [10]

Then, during the first three stages of Samadhi, even the suppressing wave becomes successively weaker.. Thus, during the first three stages of Samadhi, the mind-substance becomes transformed by fleeting experiences of Samadhi which occur during an interval between successive suppressing waves. [11]

The fourth stage of Samadhi occurs when, because the mind is so still Consciousness can focus solely on the Superconscious experience of Samadhi, each wave that arises is identical to the wave-image that just subsided. Thus, during the fourth stage of Samadhi, the mind-substance becomes transformed solely by the one wave-impression of the Superconscious experience made possible by one's attention being undivided and one-pointed. [12]

❀   *T*his explanation of the successive
stages of transformation that occurs
within the mind-substance during the three practices
which allows you to Become the Object also explains
the sequence of transformation that occurs over time
within all physical objects that are composed of
neutrons, protons and electrons, and which can be
perceived by the senses; and explains how particular
characteristics of objects can only be described in
terms of an event that appears in a frozen state of
animation within separate, individual space-time
frames; and in terms of which time frame is being
viewed. [13]

All of the characteristics of an object that appear over a period of time—characteristics which appear in time-frames that have disappeared into the past; characteristics which can be seen in present time-frames; and future characteristics which have not yet arisen—are inherent in the subtle level of matter which composes the gross physical form from the beginning, and which only arise under particular circumstances and conditions. [14]

Different visible characteristics that appear as changes in brain cells and external behavior patterns, which can be seen arising in successive space-time frames, are merely outer manifestations of a transformation that has occurred on the opposite, inner, psychological level of the mind. [15]

❀   *T*hrough the practice of Becoming the Object of the orderly sequence of transformation that occurs within the mind-substance over periods of time as the result of the three practices of Concentration, Meditation and Samadhi; and gain an understanding of how sequential changes take place, you will gain personal knowledge of the transformations that will become visable within the mind-substance in the future. [16]

❀ *T*hrough the practice of Becoming the Object of the difference between the mind hearing a particular combination of sound vibrations; putting those vibrations together into a word that denotes an object, which then appears as a visual image on the mind-screen; and subsequent ideas about that object that arise from memory, based on past experience and beliefs—three separate mental functions which, because they occur so rapidly, become superimposed upon each other and thus are usually experienced as a single event—you will be able to understand the meaning of any sound produced by any living creature. [17]

You will also be able to directly perceive the impressions that are stored within the mind of any creature, and come to know the past actions of that soul which were the origin of his or her present birth, circumstances, life span, and experiences of pleasure and pain; [18]

And by analyzing the mental images that are presently appearing on the surface of his or her mind, you will understand why the events of the present are occurring. [19]

❀   Conversely, you can sever the mental link between yourself and any object created of the five natural elements that is within the range of the senses. [20]

❀   *T*hrough the practice of Becoming the Object of the point where the light that is reflected off of the physical body you are looking at meets your eyes power of perception, you will be able to suspend your visual awareness so that any object, or portion of any object, will dissolve and disappear from your sight; enabling you to look into, or through, any gross physical form. [21]

This explains how you can also suspend awareness of the sensations of sound, taste, smell and touch while you continue to remain involved in outer physical activities. [22]

❀   *T*hrough the practice of Becoming the
Object of the orderly succession of
karma that is presentlya rising in relation to latent
karma that has not yet taken form, you will gain an
understanding of the circumstances that will occur
near the end of life, and recognize the omens and
portents that will signal the oncoming of this last
event of this birth. [23]

However, difficulties that are destined to arise can be
modified by increasing your expression of the Four
Virtues of friendliness, compassion, delight and non-
attached empathy, for the inner strength you will gain
through increasing these virtues will help to soften
painful karma; [24]

And through increasing your expression of the other virtues as well, you will gain strength equal to that of an elephant, and thus be able to more easily endure that which would otherwise be experienced as a great hardship; $_{25}$

And, by directing your Inner Light of Consciousness outward, you will gain an understanding about things that are as small as an atom, as concealed as buried treasure, and as remote in space and time as the farthermost galaxies, and thereby protect yourself from influences that cannot normally be perceived. $_{26}$

❀ *T*hrough the practice of Becoming the Object of the hot, dry, self-luminous sun, symbol of the masculine Pranic Life Energy that runs along the right side of the spine and body, you will gain personal knowledge of the earth and the other planets of the solar system that encircle the sun; [27]

And through the practice of Becoming the Object of the cool, moist, reflective moon that controls the tides of life, symbol of the feminine Pranic Life Energy that runs along the left side of the spine and body, you will gain personal knowledge of the arrangement of the star constellations across which the moon moves on her monthly path around the earth; [28]

And through the practice of Becoming the Object of the brilliant light of the Pole Star, located where the Northern extension of the earth's axis pierces the sky, symbol of the Light of Consciousness at the top of the head at the central axis of the body—which transcends the complementary opposites of masculine and feminine, yet contains within itself the opposites of both—you will gain personal knowledge of the course of the sun, moon and all of the heavenly bodies which appear to revolve around the central, unmoving point of the light of the Pole Star. [29]

Chapter Three

❁   *T*hen practice Becoming the
Object of the bodily counterparts of
the sun, moon and Pole Star:

Through the practice of placing your Center of Consciousness in the third chakra, counterpart of the
world navel, and Becoming the Object of the qualities
of the third chakra— source of the outgoing masculine qualities of will, assertiveness, intellect and
logic—you will become the embodiment of these
dynamic qualities, and gain personal knowledge of
the arrangement of the internal organs that encircle
this chakra just as the planets encircle the sun; $_{30}$

And through the practice of placing your Center of
Consciousness in the throat center and Becoming the
Object of the qualities of the fifth chakra—source of
the intaking feminine qualities of love, receptivity,
emotions and intuition—you will become the embodiment of these passive qualities of love, and thus will
cease to thirst for these outside of yourself; $_{31}$

And through the practice of lowering your Center of
Consciousness downwards, and Becoming the Object
of the qualities of the mythological deep sea tortoise,

Kurma, upon whose back rests the lower axis of the revolving earth; and through Becoming the Object of the central, unmoving central axis of the body; you will gain personal knowledge of the central nerve channel that runs through the center of the spine. This main central nerve channel has its basis in the primitive forms of life at the bottom of the sea, experienced through the lower chakras, and culminates in the Light of Divine Consciousness at the crown center of the head; which transcends even the higher forms of life, and which forms the central axis of the dynamic, revolving spheres of the Worlds of the Chakras, and is the axis around which the masculine and feminine, positive and negative, Pranic Energies intertwine and become joined—all of which underlie and support your gross physical form. [32]

❀   *T*hen, through the practice of raising your Center of Consciousness up through the central nerve channel and Becoming the Object of the Supernormal Vision that one attains when ones Consciousness enters the Effulgent Light in the sixth chakra at the center of the forehead, your ability to clearly see the presence of the Divinity everywhere will become perfect; [33]

And when you gain the ability to raise your Center of Consciousness up through the central nerve channel and Become the Object of the Light of Consciousness that lies above the earthly worlds in the seventh chakra at the crown center of the head, you will become the embodiment of the Power of all of the facets of Supernormal Divine Perception. [34]

103

Chapter Three

❀   **N**ext, through the practice of placing your Center of Consciousness in the fourth chakra in the heart, and Becoming the Object of its dual sets of qualities, you will become aware that the heart is the home of the mind. Since the heart is situated between the primitive worlds of the first, second and third chakras below—in which are experienced and acted out the compulsive instinctual drives, fears and egoistic tendencies; and the more mature evolved worlds of the Fifth, Sixth and Seventh Chakras above the heart—in which are experienced and acted out the power of choice, compassion and love; you will see that the heart can serve the purposes of either the self-focused motives of the lower chakras, or the other-focused motives of the centers of Consciousness above. 35

Then, through raising your Center of Consciousness up through the center of the spine to the seventh chakra in the crown center at the top of the head, and Becoming the Object of your Conscious True-Self, you will see that it is your True-Self which is Self-Luminous like the sun, while the Lake of the Mind is merely a transparent, reflective substance which, like the ever-changing moon, reflects both the Light, Bliss and Peace of the chakras above the heart, as well as the darkness, passion and suffering that can be experienced in the lower chakras. When you understand that Consciousness is completely and absolutely separate from this mind-substance, and that It never becomes mixed with the mental processes, you will know that the higher purpose of the mind is to serve your True-Self, rather than merely serving as a mirror which reflects sensory impressions of the external world and the experiences of pleasure and pain which arise from impressions of ignorance when Consciousness is identified there. [36]

❀ *A*fter you have become aware of the difference between the mind and Consciousness, in addition to spontaneously and instantly knowing everything you need to know, the Power of Divine Seeing, Hearing, Smelling, Tasting and Feeling will also be born within you. ₃₇

 But beware! Do not develop an inflated ego because you have been given access to these Divine Powers because if you do, it will create obstacles which will eclipse the Inner Light of Consciousness and prevent you from reaching the seventh chakra and attaining the highest degree of Divine Bliss and Happiness, that only comes through experiencing the fifth Samadhi. ₃₈

But if you have left behind all ego desires to exhibit these powers, you may project your Consciousness outwards and enter into the solid physical body of others, perceive the causes of suffering that are stored in their mind, and help them to attain a permanent state of happiness and peace while they are still in a body here on earth. ₃₉

Chapter Three

❀　　　Since you will now be the Master of the forces of nature, by controlling the upward flowing Pranic Life Energy—which counter-acts the forces of gravity in order that the bodily fluids and energies may circulate upwards—you will be able to walk on water, float above mud, rise above sharp objects, and so on; [40]

And by controlling the Pranic Life Energy which heats and digests food, and provides warmth for the body, your body temperature will increase to a blazing radiance. [41]

❀   *B*y Becoming the Object of the Power of Hearing, and binding it to the ether that pervades space, you will be able to hear the Divine sound, OM. [42]

And by Becoming the Object of your physical body, and binding it to the ether that pervades space, you will be able to separate your subtle body from your gross physical body and, since your subtle body weighs less than a feather, move unimpeded through space. [43]

❀   Separating your subtle physical body
from your gross physical body is
completely different from the mere sensation of
floating, levitating, and dissolving into space that was
previously described as occurring during the breathing practices. While those sensations were imaginary,
a true out-of-body experience is real, and you will
know with all certainty that you are not imagining it.
This great happening, through which you gain the
understanding that you, as Eternal Consciousness, are
not in any way dependent on the physical body,
causes a marvelous enlightening wave to wash over
your mind, which sweeps away the impressions
caused by ignorance of this fact which had obstructed
your vision of the inner Light. 44

❀ *T*hen, through Becoming the Object of the profound purpose of Consciousness having become the four levels of matter from subtle to gross; and of the purpose of the four levels of matter linking together to form your body; you will become aware that you, Consciousness, are the master of the five natural elements that compose the objective world. ₄₅

At this moment, the Eight Highest Powers of Perfection will become alive within you, so that you will be able to contract your Consciousness and become smaller than the nucleus of an atom; expand your Consciousness and become as vast as the totality of the cosmos; go to any location in the universe; control any event; create, change or dissolve gross physical objects; and fulfill any wish; without destroying or harming the outer observable characteristics of your body. ₄₆

In fact, the body of a Perfected Being, who is a visible form of the Power of Divine Consciousness, is graceful, strong and energetic, and capable of dispelling and destroying any disease or karma of others that enters into it, and thus remain intact. ₄₇

❀   *T*hrough Becoming the Object of the significance of the permanent cognitive process that has continually observed and redefined who, and what, you are, based on your personal experience of the successively more subtle levels of matter— which corresponds to successively more expanded levels of Consciousness, Divine Truth and Blissful Love—you will know that you are the Conscious-Seer who is perceiving the universe, and that Consciousness is the Master of the senses and the mind. [48]

This explains why the most excellent of Perfected Beings are able to separate their Consciousness from their instrument of the body, mind and senses and, as Consciousness alone, rapidly move through space with full awareness of sights, sounds, smells, tastes and touch. [49]

❀ *T*hrough becoming aware that there is a vast difference between the diluted experience of peace, joy and blissful love that is a reflection of the True-Self that can be known through a purified mind; and the direct undiluted experience of Peace, Joy and Blissful Love that is the very essence of the Consciousness of the True-Self, which can only be known through direct contact during the states of Samadhi, the power of Supreme, Unwavering All-Knowingness will arise within you. [50]

As a result of gaining this understanding that there is a difference between the wonderful, though impermanent happiness, that is experienced through the mind and senses; and the permanent, and completely different and incomparably beautiful experience of ones True-Self, the seeds of desire, anger, fear and depression that had produced painful, agitated states of mind, and kept you bound to the world, will become weak, and then you will be able to separate yourself from them. 51

But once again, beware! If you develop pride and become impressed with yourself because you have been invited to become a member of a community of adepts, the expression of your smile will reveal the true disposition of your mind, and you will find that this ominous evil inclination will cause you to become caught in nature's trap once again. 52

❀ *B*y Becoming the Object of the orderly succession of infinitesimal quantum moments of time, beyond which no further division can take place—the duration of which is determined by the smallest space/time movement of sub atomic matter from one point to another—indicating the smallest degree of the decay and transformation of matter—you will gain personal knowledge that time in itself does not exist except as an eternal present, and that past and future is only a mental concept used to describe the transformation of matter. Then you will gain the ability to stand apart and observe matter within 'time' as it passes within quantum time-frames from its present, to its future, mutations. [53]

This will enable you to distinguish the difference between objects that appear to be identical in species, outer characteristics, and position in space and time that ordinarily could not be distinguished between. [54]

Once you gain this degree of discrimination between one space/time frame and another, you will transcend the barrier of space/time sequences, and instantly, and simultaneously, know the past, present and possible future mutations of all objects and events in the universe that are composed of neutrons, protons and electrons, at every moment of their existence, and in all of their past, present and future modifications, and thus transcend the limitation of perceiving events as incomplete, fragmented time-frames. [55]

❀ When only the Light of the Conscious ness of your True-Self pervades your mind, so that your mind is equal in purity to the One Self which dwells within you as you, you will live in the world completely independent from the usual limitations of the mind. 56

Chapter Four

✿   Occasionally a rare soul is born in whom the Divine Powers of Perfection arise spontaneously, without him or her having practiced any spiritual disciplines, as the result of spiritual attainments in past lives. In all cases, however, the Divine Powers of Perfection are always preceded at some point—in this or in a former life—by one having:

> *Purified the body* through proper diet and medicinal herbs;
>
> *Steadied the mind* through repetition of a name of God;
>
> *Strengthened the mind* through self-discipline; and
>
> *Transformed the mind* through experiencing Truth directly during the states of Samadhi. ₁

As a result of practicing these disciplines, a soul evolves from one birth to the next until the mind becomes purified and transformed back into the basic matter of nature during the fourth stage of Samadhi, when, because one has become one with the Divine Love and Bliss that is experienced at the level of the Unified Field of the universe, one knows, 'All of This is Me.' [2]

The practices themselves, however, are not the direct cause of the mind-substance becoming transformed back into the Unified Field to its original state of purity, nor are they the direct cause of the Powers of Perfection. The practices only remove the obstacles from the mind-field that are obstructing the outward flow of Consciousness, just as when a farmer removes the obstacles from the irrigation ditches in his field, the water from the reservoir, no longer held back, flows naturally forward. [3]

All psychological obstacles in the mind-field are created by the single belief, 'I am my body and mind'. [4]

118

Although throughout countless lives the transmigrating soul pursues many diverse sensory and emotional activities and experiences based on the belief that it is its body and mind, the director of all of these various pursuits, and the mind-substance within which the karmic impressions of these experiences and reactions are recorded, remaineds the same throughout all one's births. ₅

The only outer activity that a soul can pursue that does not infect the mind with an accumulation of karmic impressions that cause rebirth is the practice of meditation. ₆

Thus, those who are practicing the disciplines of this psychology are learning how not to accumulate either good or bad karmic impressions, while others are continuing to accumulate impressions in the mind that produce three kinds of karma: good, bad, and mixed. ₇

As these karmic impressions ripen, they produce particular rebirths that will provide the conditions and circumstances within which one can pursue one's unfulfilled desires and interests. ₈

119

Although a soul's births are separated, one from the other, by long periods of time, distant locations, and by rebirth into different species, there is no interruption in the sequential manifestation of karma, because the mind-substance that contains the impressions, and the memory that recognizes them, are the same. [9]

The Law of Karma that produces rebirth in order to connect causes to effects is an eternal Divine Cosmic Principle. [10]

❀   *T*here is, however, a way to end the cycles of cause and effect that produce the closed loop of the pleasure and pain of death and rebirth. Since causes and effects are bound together in order to connect a sensation to its cause, if the cause ceases to exist, the effect will also cease to exist. [11]

All mental characteristics which have manifested in the past, and all possible characteristics which can manifest in the future, have existed in potential form within one's own mind since the beginning. Thus, because of the Law of Cause and Effect, the characteristics that will arise and become visible in the future will depend upon which road you travel in the present. [12]

The different characteristics that will manifest on the visible, physical level of brain cells depend upon the nature of the different impressions you accumulate in the mind-substance due to your life-style and pursuits, which determine whether the impressions you collect are inert, ignorant and dark; active, passionate and red; or peaceful, happy and clear. [13]

All creatures in the universe evolve as, one by one, the nature of the impressions in the subtle mind-substance—which are stored in the cells of the brain—become transformed from ignorance to passion, and from passion to peace and happiness. [14]

The degree to which any mind is able to perceive the characteristics of an object accurately is equal to the degree that one has separated the impressions in the mind from each other, examined them one by one, and altered them by a change in life-style, pursuits and attitudes. [15]

Thus, the criteria of whether any object possesses certain characteristics or not cannot be based on the evaluation of a single mind, because if that mind did not perceive the characteristics accurately, what would happen to the object? [16]

Different people perceive the same object differently. This is because one can only understand an object in terms of which characteristics that particular mind is able to perceive and understand. [17]

Chapter Four

In contrast, the Lord of the Mind, one's inner Conscious-Self, has accurate knowledge of all of the characteristics of objects because thought-waves in the mind-substance do not effect the Conscious-Self; [18]

While the mind, having no Consciousness of its own, is seen to be merely a luminous surface across which flows rippling wave-images . [19]

Unlike one's True-Self, which is Conscious both of Itself and the objects it perceives, the mind is not even Conscious of itself. In fact, like a computer and its programs, it cannot even function unless Consciousness is connected to it. [20]

If one were to postulate that there is no unchanging, Conscious True-Self who is the Seer, and that the mind-substance itself is what perceives, then when one's mind perceived a second mind of a second soul, a third mind of a third soul, and so on in an infinite regression, the mind would be confused as to which memories and inclinations were its own, and thus one would lack a sense of continuity and identity. [21]

One does not lack a sense of continuity and identity, however, because of the presence of an unchanging Conscious Observer. Thus, even though Pure Consciousness is understanding sequential space-time events and states of relationship in terms of the way they appear when viewed through the lens of the internal instrument of the mind, Pure Consciousness Itself does not mix with mental events, even though It may be currently identifying with them. [22]

Thus, although Consciousness Itself does not mix with the events in the mind, since the mind reflects both the Light of the Conscious-Self from above and the shapes and colors of objects that are appearing on its surface from below, it appears to the Light of the Conscious-Self that It is the shapes, colors and events It is seeing. [23]

This association between Consciousness, and the innumerable impressions in the mind, is the cause of rebirth. But there is another special, and distinctly different, purpose of the mind. [24]

Chapter Four

The special purpose of the mind-substance is to become a reflective, third dimensional surface, which is completely smooth and free of mind-waves, so that the Eternal, Conscious True-Self can see an undistorted vision of Its own Divine Light. [25]

Then it becomes easy to discriminate between the Light of one's own Consciousness, and the impressions which are borne within the mind-substance, and so one is naturally inclined to remain separate from the processes in the mind. [26]

However, through the force they accumulated over many lives, past impressions that create obstacles may still at times invade the mind during intervals when you are not remembering to discriminate between your Self, Consciousness, and the thoughts in your mind. [27]

When this happens, you must regain the power of discrimination and remove the causes of suffering from your mind in the manner that was previously described. [28]

After your awareness has been made pure and clear during the fourth stage of Samadhi, if you continue to discriminate between your Conscious-Self, and the experience of Divine Truth/Consciousness/Bliss that accompanies the fourth stage of Samadhi when you realize, 'All of This is Me', and remain aware that even the Love and Bliss that is experienced at the level of the Unified Field of the universe is still but a rarefied level of physical matter, and a diluted experience of your True-Self; and thus remain disinterested in identifying even with this most rare and exalted experience; you will pass through the rarefied matter of the Unified Field of the universe, called the 'Cloud of Forms', transcend the third dimension of space, time and matter, and enter into the fifth stage of Samadhi that is in the dimension that lies on the other side of the Cloud of Forms; [29]

Where the causes of suffering, and the karma associated with them, do not exist. [30]

✿   *T*hus, with your mind now unswept by intellectual, emotional, sensory or memory currents, you escape the limitations of the third dimensional universe of forms, and enter the strata of Infinity during this fifth and highest stage of Samadhi. The pure, undiluted experience of this ultimate dimension of the Love and Power of the Spiritual Reality is so far greater than the most exalted of third dimensional experiences that there is little that can be said about it. [31]

Now that you have fulfilled the purpose of life, the sequence of the transformation of the triad of sub atomic particles that compose your mind has come to an end. [32]

With your awareness now centered in the Still Point of Eternity, in the Spiritual Dimension where time and change do not exist, you transcend the limitation of fragmented views of space-time events, and instantaneously and simultaneously become aware of all past, and possible future, events. This indicates that when the present life comes to an end, your journeys through the ever-changing illusory third dimensional world of space, time and matter have come to an end. [33]

Chapter Four

Since the triad of neutrons, protons and electrons which composed the subtle mind-substance have now been reversed back into their original, non-differentiated state, one's True Conscious-Self separates Itself completely from the World of Nature, and, through Its own Power, flows into the totality of Its own Pure Consciousness. [34]

❀

*Sanskrit/English
Transliteration and Translations*

Chapter One

1. atha *(now)*; yoga *(yoga psychology)*; anushasanam *(instruction)*.

2. yogas *(mystical union attained)*; chitta *(mind-substance)*; vritti *(thought-waves)*; nirodhah *(suppress)*.

3. tada *(then)*; drashtuh *(desires to see)*; svarupe *(own form)*; avasthanam *(remains in and exhibits)*.

4. vritti *(thought-waves)*; sarupyam *(with those forms)*; itaratra *(at other times)*.

5. vrittayah *(thought-waves)*; pancha *(five)*; tayyah *(types)*; klishta *(produce mental and emotional suffering)*; aklishta *(do not produce mental and emotional suffering)*.

6. pramana *(correct understanding)*; viparyaya *(incorrect understanding)*; vikalpa *(imagination)*; nidra *(deep dreamless sleep)*; smritayah *(memory)*.

7. pratyaksha *(direct perception)*; anumana *(logical conclusion)*; agama *(scriptural verification)*; pramanani *(correct understanding)*.

8. viparyayah *(incorrect understanding)*; mithya *(false)*; jnanam *(accurate personal knowledge)*; atad *(not that)*; rupa *(form)*; pratishtham *(rest in)*.

9. shabda *(has heard)*; jnana *(accurate personal knowledge)*; anupati *(following upon)*; vastu *(any existing thing)*; shunyo *(void)*; vikalpah *(imagination)*.

10. abhava *(not born)*; pratyaya *(thought process)*; alambana *(sensation connected with its cause)*; vrittir *(thought waves)*; nidra *(deep dreamless sleep)*.

11. anubhuta *(connected with the five elements)*; vishaya *(objects of the senses composed of neutrons, protons and electrons)*; asampramoshah *(not forgotten)*; smritih *(memory)*.

12. abhyasa *(practice)*; vairagya *(emotionally free from agitation and suffering caused by desire and fear)*; bhyam *(by)*; tat *(that)*; nirodhah *(suppress)*.

13. tatra *(in that)*; sthitau *(steady)*; yatnah *(effort)*; abhyasah *(practice to form the habit)*.

14. sah *(it)*; tu *(but)*; dirgha *(long)*; kala *(time)*; nairantarya *(without interruption or interval)*; satkara *(positive attitude)*; asevitah *(persistence)*; dridha *(unwavering)*; bhumih *(grounded)*.

15. drishta *(looked at)*; anushravika *(heard about)*; vishaya *(objects of the senses composed of neutrons, protons and electrons)*; vitrishnasya *(not thirst)*; vasikara *(mastery)*; samjna *(has recovered consciousness)*; vairagyam *(emotionally free from agitation and suffering caused by desire and fear)*.

16. tat *(that)*; param *(highest)*; purusha *(True-Self)*; khyater *(awareness of)*; guna *(triad of neutrons, protons and electrons)*; vaitrishnyam *(not thirst)*.

17. vitarka *(logical examination)*; vichara *(reflective contemplation)*; ananda *(divine bliss)*; asmita *(I am all of this)*; anugamat *(connected with)*; samprajnatah *(enlightened intelligence and wisdom)*.

18. virama *(terminated)*; pratyaya *(thought process)*; abhyasa *(practice)*; purvah *(previous)*; samskara *(impression)*; seshah *(undefiled)*; anyah *(different)*.

19. bhava *(birth)*; pratyayah *(thought process)*; videha *(with no body)*; prakriti *(basic matter of nature)*; layanam *(merge)*.

20. sraddha *(faith)*; virya *(heroism)*; smriti *(memory)*; samadhi *(expanded consciousness)*; prajna *(enlightened intelligence and wisdom)*; purvakah *(preceded)*; itaresham *(by others)*.

21. tivra *(ardent)*; sam *(with)*; veganam *(enthusiasm)*; asannah *(soon)*.

22. mridu *(mild)*; madhya *(moderate)*; adhimatratvat *(one who is most intense)*; tatah *(from that)*; api *(also)*; viseshah *(distinctly different and special)*.

23. isvara *(divine being)*; pranidhanat *(come to God with faith, devotion and surrender)*; va *(and)*.

24. klesa *(psychological causes of suffering)*; karma *(cause and effect)*; vipaka *(ripen)*; asayair *(stored)*; apara *(beyond)*; mrishtah *(mortality)*; purusha *(True-Self)*; viseshah *(distinctly different and special)*; isvarah *(divine being)*.

25. tatra *(in that)*; nir *(not is)*; atisayam *(excelled)*; sarva *(all)*; jna *(knowing)*; bijam *(seed)*.

26. sah *(it)*; purvesham *(former)*; api *(also)*; guru *(spiritual master)*; kalena *(within time)*; anavachchhedat *(cannot be distinguished between)*.

27. tasya *(that is)*; vachakah *(the word which was expressed)*; pranavah *(sound of the moment of creation)*; Om *(sound of the instant of creation)*.

28. tat *(that)*; japah *(repetition of a name of God)*; tat *(that)*; artha *(meaning and purpose)*; bhavanam *(will be born)*.

Chapter One

Sanskrit/English Translations

29. tatah *(from that);* pratyak *(direct inner perception);* chetana *(divine consciousness);* adhigamah *(attain);* api *(also);* antaraya *(inner psychological obstacles);* abhavah *(not born);* cha *(and).*

30. vyadhi *(illness);* styana *(resistance);* samsaya *(doubt);* pramada *(disinterest);* alasya *(laziness);* avirati *(not abstaining);* bhranti *(distorted);* darsana *(direct vision of the deity);* alabdha *(not gain);* bhumikatva *(grounded);* anava *(not possible);* sthitatvani *(steadiness);* chitta *(mind);* vikshepah *(distractions;* te *(these);* antarayah *(inner psychological obstacles).*

31. duhkha *(suffering);* daurmanasya *(despair, anxiety, bad disposition);* angame *(parts);* jayatva *(uncontrolled);* svasa *(inhalation);* prasvasa *(uncontrolled exhalation);* vikshepa *(distraction);* saha *(natural);* bhuvah *(accompany);.*

32. tat *(that);* pratishedha *(counteract);* artham *(purpose);* eka *(first);* tattva *(level);* abhyasah *(practice to form the habit).*

33. maitri *(friendliness);* karuna *(compassion);* mudita *(rejoicing);* upekshanam *(non-attached empathy);* sukha *(happy);* duhkha *(suffering);* punya *(virtuous);* apunya *(evil);* vishayanam *(objects of the senses composed of neutrons, protons and electrons);* bhavanatah *(will be born);* chitta *(mind-substance);* prasadanam *(clarity and pleasantness).*

34. prachchhardana *(controlled exhalation);* vidharana *(maintain outside);* bhyam *(by);* va *(and);* pranasya *(of the breath).*

35. vishaya *(objects of the senses composed of neutrons, protons and electrons);* vati *(connected to);* va *(and);* pravrittih *(outward turned mind-waves);* utpanna *(rise above);* manasah *(the mind);* sthiti *(steady);* nibandhani *(that which binds).*

36. visoka *(beyond sorrow);* va *(and);* jyotishmati *(effulgent light of your divine self).*

37. vita (*without*); raga (*mental excitement and passionate emotional agitation due to desires for certain things*); vishayam (*objects of the senses composed of neutrons, protons and electrons*); va (*and*); chittam (*mind-substance*).

38. svapna (*dream*); nidra (*deep dreamless sleep*); jnana (*accurate personal knowledge*); alambanam (*that which connects a sensation with its cause*); va (*and*).

39. yatha (*as*); abhimata (*that which one holds most dear*); dhyanat (*meditation*); va (*and*).

40. parama (*highest*); anu (*most minute*); parama (*beyond*); mahattva (*most great*); anta (*end*); asya (*one*); vasikarah (*made subject to one's will*).

41. kshina (*weaken*); vritter (*thought-waves*); abhijatasya (*transparent*); iva (*as if*); maner (*jewel*); grahitri (*knower*); grahana (*act of knowing*); grayeshu (*that which is known*); tatstha (*rests in that*); tad (*that*); anjanata (*takes that coloring*); samapattih (*fusion with*).

42. tatra (*in that*); sabda (*has heard*); artha (*meaning*); jnana (*accurate personal knowledge*); vikalpaih (*imagination*); samkirna (*intermingle*); savitarka (*with logical examination*).

43. smriti (*memory*); parisuddhau (*ultimate state of purity*); svarupa (*own form*); sunya (*void*); iva (*as if*); artha (*meaning*); matra (*sum total*); nirbhasa (*shines forth*); nirvitarka (*without logical examination*).

44. etaya (*by this*); eva (*only*); savichara (*with reflective contemplation*); nirvichara (*without reflective contemplation*); cha (*and*); sukshma (*subtle*); vishaya (*object of the senses composed of neutrons, protons and electrons*); vyakhyata (*is explained*).

45. sukshma *(subtle)*; vishayatvam *(province of objects of the senses)*; cha *(and)*; alinga *(undifferentiated)*; paryavasanam *(beyond impressions which produce rebirth)*.

46. ta *(thus)*; eva *(also)*; sabijah *(with seed)*; samadhih *(expanded states of consciousness)*.

47. nirvichara *(without reflective contemplation)*; vaisaradye *(brightness that reflects the wholeness of parts)*; adhyatma *(essence of one's own True-Self)*; prasadah *(clarity)*.

48. ritam *(supreme undiluted truth of universal divine laws)*; bhara *(bearing)*; tatra *(in that)*; prajna *(enlightened intelligence and wisdom)*.

49. sruta *(heard)*; anumana *(logical conclusion)*; prajna *(enlightened intelligence and wisdom)*; bhyam *(by)*; anya *(different)*; vishaya *(objects of the senses composed of neutrons, protons and electrons)*; visesha *(distinctly different and special)*; arthatvat *(its true meaning)*.

50. tajjah *(of that born)*; samskarah *(impression)*; anya *(different)*; samskara *(impressions)*; pratibandhi *(obstructs and prevents)*.

51. tasya *(that)*; api *(also)*; nirodhe *(suppressed)*; sarva *(all)*; nirodhan *(suppress)*; nirbijah *(without seeds)*; samadhi *(expanded states of consciousness)*.

Chapter Two

1. tapah *(self-discipline);* svadhyaya *(meditation on one's own mind);* isvara *(divine being);* pranidhanani *(mentally and emotionally surrendered to, and focused on);* kriya *(motions);* yogah *(for yoga psychology).*

2. samadhi *(expanded states of consciousness);* bhavana *(become);* artha *(purpose);* klesa *(psychological causes of suffering);* tanu *(reduce);* karana *(the activity that caused);* arthah *(purpose);* cha *(and).*

3. avidya *(ignorance);* asmita *(I-am-this);* raga *(mental excitement and passionate emotional agitation due to desires for certain things);* dvesha *(mental excitement and passionate emotional agitation due to aversions to certain things);* abhiniveshah *(tenacious determination to achieve this purpose);* klesah *(cause of psychological suffering).*

4. avidya *(ignorance);* kshetram *(field);* uttaresham *(for the others);* prasupta *(dormant);* tanu *(weak);* vichchhinna *(intercepted);* udaranam *(rising up and active).*

5. anitya *(not eternal);* asuchi *(not pure);* duhkha *(not happy);* anatmasu *(the corporeal body void of spirit);* nitya *(eternal);* suchi *(pure);* sukha *(happy);* atma *(true-self);* khyatir *(the idea);* avidya *(ignorance).*

6. drig (Seer); darsana (direct vision of the deity); saktyor (power); ekatmata (blend together as one identity); iva (as if); asmita (I-am-this).

7. sukha (happiness); anusayi (consequence of); ragah (mental excitement and passionate emotional agitation due to desires for certain things).

8. duhkha (pain and suffering); anusayi (consequence of); dveshah (mental excitement and passionate emotional agitation due to aversions to certain things).

9. svarasa (innate love of pleasure); vahi (flows); vidusho (defile); api (even); tatha (that); rudho (implanted); abhinivesah (tenacious determination to achieve this purpose).

10. te (these); pratiprasava (reverse the flow back to the original state); heyah (refuse to accept); sukshmah (subtle).

11. dhyana (meditation); heyas (refuse to accept); tad (these); vrittayah (mind-waves).

12. klesa (psychological causes of suffering); mulah (root); karma (cause and effect); asayah (stored); drishta (looked at); adrishta (not seen); janma (lives); vedaniyah (will be experienced).

13. sati (exist); mule (root); tad (that); vipakah (ripen); jati (birth in a particular species); ayuh (life span); bhogah (experiences of physical and emotional pleasure and pain) .

14. te (they); hlada (cool, refreshing, delightful); paritapa (hot, tormenting, difficult); phalah (fruit of); punya (virtuous); apunya (vice); hetutvat (will produce).

15. parinama *(transformation)*; tapa *(tormenting)*; samskara *(impression)*; duhkhair *(pain and suffering)*; guna *(three sub atomic particles)*; vritti *(mind-waves)*; virodhat *(conflict)*; cha *(and)*; duhkam *(pain and suffering)*; eva *(also)*; sarvam *(all)*; vivekinah *(analyze)*.

16. heyam *(refuse to accept)*; duhkham *(pain and suffering)*; anagatam *(not yet begun to flow)*.

17. drashtri *(the Seer)*; drisyayoh *(seen)*; samyogah *(joined to)*; heya *(refuse to accept)*; hetuh *(cause)*.

18. prakasa *(illumination)*; kriya *(motion)*; sthiti *(stillness)*; silam *(qualities)*; bhuta *(the gross physical forms in the universe composed of the five natural elements)*; indriya *(senses)*; atmakam *(consisting)*; bhoga *(experience of physical and emotional pleasure and pain)*; apavarga *(emancipation from bodily existence)*; artham *(purpose)*; drisyam *(having seen)*.

19. visesha *(distinctly different and special)*; avisesha *(not different, distinct or special)*; linga *(with qualities)*; matra *(sum total)*; alingani *(without qualities)*; guna *(three building blocks of nature)*; parvani *(stages of development)*.

20. drashta *(the Seer)*; drisimatrah *(the amount that is seen)*; shudda *(pure and clear)*; api *(although)*; pratyaya *(thought process)*; anupasyah *(appears to be)*.

21. tad *(that)*; artha *(meaning)*; eva *(also)*; drisyasya *(having seen)*; atma *(True-self)*.

22. krita *(fulfill)*; artham *(purpose)*; prati *(by reversing)*; nashtam *(is destroyed)*; api *(although)*; anashtam *(not destroyed)*; tat *(that)*; anya *(different)*; sadharanatvat *(who are concentrated on it)*.

23. sva *(own)*; svami *(owner, master)*; saktyoh *(power)*; svarupa *(own form)*; upalabdhi *(the appearance of)*; hetuh *(cause)*; samyogah *(united with)*.

24. tasya *(this)*; hetur *(cause)*; avidya *(ignorance)*.

25. tad *(that)*; abhavat *(disappears)*; samyoga *(identity with)*; abhavah *(disappears)*; hanam *(removal of)*; tat *(that)*; driseh *(the seen)*; kaivalyam *(separated from)*.

26. viveka *(analysis)*; khyatih *(awareness)*; aviplava *(unwavering)*; hana *(remove)*; upayah *(the means)*.

27. tashya *(in this way)*; saptadha *(sevenfold)*; pranta *(last)*; bhumih *(become grounded in)*; prajna *(intelligence and wisdom)*.

28. yoga *(mystical union)*; anga *(steps)*; anushthanat *(by carrying out)*; asuddhi *(impurities)*; kshaye *(diminish)*; jnana *(accurate personal knowledge)*; diptih *(light)*; a *(up)*; viveka *(analysis)*; khyateh *(aware of)*.

29. yama *(restraints; five virtues for happy relationships)*; niyama *(observances; five virtues for happy personal life)*; asana *(sitting posture)*; pranayama *(control the breath)*; pratyahara *(turning the senses inward)*; dharana *(concentration)*; dhyana *(meditation)*; samadhi *(expanded states of consciousness)*; ashta *(eight)*; angani *(steps)*.

30. ahimsa *(do not be violent, angry or aggressive)*; satya *(do not lie)*; asteya *(do not steal)*; brahmacharya *(do not lust over others)*; aparigrahah *(do not amass possessions or accept gifts with strings attached)*; yamah *(restraints; five virtues for happy relationships)*.

31. jati *(birth into a particular species)*; desa *(location)*; kala *(time)*; samaya *(coming together)*; anavachchhinnah *(unbounded)*; sarva *(all)*; bhaumah *(levels)*; maha *(greatest)*; vratam *(vow)*.

32. saucha *(purity)*; samtosha *(contentment)*; tapah *(self-discipline)*; svadhyaya *(meditation on one's mind)*; isvara *(divine being)*; pranidhanani *(mentally and emotionally surrendered to, and focused on)*; niyamah *(observances; five virtues for happy personal life)*.

33. vitarka *(thinking)*; badhane *(disturbing)*; pratipaksha *(prevent by reversing to the opposite)*; bhavanam *(come into being)*.

34. vitarka *(thinking)*; himsadayah *(violence done by oneself)*; krita *(fulfilled)*; karita *(cause to be done)*; anumoditah *(approve of it being done)*; lobha *(greed)*; krodha *(anger)*; moha *(delusion)*; purvakah *(preceded by)*; mridu *(mild)*; madhya *(moderate)*; adhimatrah *(intense)*; duhkha *(pain and suffering)*; ajnana *(not accurate personal knowledge)*; ananta *(endless)*; phalah *(fruit)*; iti *(thus)*; pratipaksha *(prevent by reversing to the opposite)*; bhavanam *(bring into being)*.

35. ahimsa *(non-violence)*; pratishthayam *(resting in the opposite of)*; tat *(that)*; samnidhau *(presence of)*; vaira *(conflict)*; tyagah *(abandon)*.

36. satya *(truthfulness)*; pratishthayam *(resting in the opposite of)*; kriya *(activity)*; phala *(result)*; asrayatvam *(basis of)*.

37. asteya *(not stealing,)*; pratishthayam *(resting in the opposite of)*; sarva *(all)*; ratna *(jewels)*; upasthanam *(abide with)*.

38. brahmacharya *(continence)*; pratishthayam *(resting in the opposite of)*; virya *(hero)*; labhah *(gain)*.

39. aparigraha *(renounce amassing possessions, and accepting gifts with strings attached)*; sthairye *(motionless)*; janma *(births)*; kathamta *(answers how and why)*; sambodhah *(perfect enlightened understanding)*.

40. sauchat *(by attaining purity)*; svanga *(parts of one's own body)*; jugupsa *(indifferent)*; paraih *(distant)*; asamsargah *(will not want contact with)*.

41. sattva *(light,joy and peace)*; suddhi *(purity)*; saumanasya *(cheerful mind)*; ekagrya *(closely attentive)*; indria *(senses)*; jaya *(victory)*; atma *(true-self)*; darsana*(direct vision of the deity)*; yogyatvani *(capable of Mystical Union)*; cha*(and)*.

42. samtoshat *(contentment)*; anuttaman *(unsurpassed)*; sukha *(happiness)*; labhah *(gain)*.

43. kaya *(body)*; indriya *(senses)*; siddhi *(perfection)*; asuddhi *(impurities)*; kshayat *(decrease)*; tapasah.*(burn up, self-directed discipline)*.

44. svadhyayad *(self-directed meditation and sanalysis of one's own mind)*; ishtadevata *(one's chosen form of God)*; samprayogah *(will be united with)*.

45. samadhi *(expanded states of consciousness)*; siddhir *(perfection)*; isvara *(divine being)*; pranidhanat*(self-surrender and coming close to God with faith, devotion and surrender)*.

46. sthira *(steady)*; sukham *(happy)*; asanam *(in the seated posture)*.

47. prayatna *(willful effort)*; saithilya *(lessen)*; ananta *(endless)*; samapattibhyam *(will become one with)*.

48. tato *(after that)*; dvandva *(opposites)*; anabhighatah *(will not disturb)*.

49. tasmin *(in this)*; sati *(exists)*; svasa *(inhalation)*; prasvasayor *(controlled exhalation)*; gati *(movement)*; vichchhedah *(that which is in between)*; pranayama *(breath control)*.

50. bahya *(external)*; abhyantara *(internal)*; stambah *(stop)*; vrittir *(mind-waves)*; desa *(place)*; kala *(time)*; samkhyabhih *(number)*; paridrishto *(regulated)*; dirgha *(long)*; sukshmah *(subtle)*.

51. bahya *(external)*; abhyantara *(internal)*; vishaya *(objects composed of neutrons, protons and electrons)*; akshepi *(transcending)*; chaturthah *(has been explained)*.

52. tatah *(from that)*; kshiyati *(dissolves)*; prakasa *(effulgence)*; avaranam *(covering)*.

53. dharanasu *(through concentration)*; cha *(and)*; yogyata *(becomes fit for mystical union)*; manasah*(of the mind)*.

54. sva *(own);* vishaya *(object composed of neutrons, protons and electrons);* asamprayoga *(sever the link);* chitta *(mind-substance);* svarupa *(own form);* anukara *(resembles);* iva *(like);* indriyanam *(when the senses);* pratyaharah *(turning the senses inward).*

55. tatah *(from that);* parama *(highest);* vasyata *(obedient to your will);* indriyanam *(senses).*

Chapter Three

1. desa *(place)*; bandhah *(bind)*; chittasya *(mind-substance)*; dharana *(concentration)*.

2. tatra *(in that)*; pratyaya *(thought process)*; eka *(one)*; tanata *(unbroken)*; dhyanam *(meditation)*.

3. tad *(that)*; eva *(also)*; arthamatra *(the height, depth, breadth, length)*; nirbhasam *(shining with)*; svarupa *(own form)*; sunyam *(void)*; iva *(as if)*; samadhih*(expanded states of consciousness)*.

4. trayam *(these three)*; ekatra *(one after one)*; samyamah *(becoming the object)*.

5. tat *(these)*; jayat *(mastery)*; prajna *(enlightened intelligence and wisdom)*; lokah *(shining forth)*.

6. tasya *(it)*; bhumishu *(in stages)*; viniyogah *(accomplish union)*.

7. trayam *(these three)*; antara *(inner)*; angam *(steps)*; purve *(previous)*; bhyah *(from)*.

8. tat *(these)*; api *(also)*; bahir *(outer)*; angam *(steps)*; nirbijasya *(in relation to seedless)*.

9. vyutthana *(outward pursuing)*; nirodha *(suppress)*; samskarayoh *(these recorded impressions)*; abhibhava *(overpower)*; pradur *(visible)*; bhavau *(come into being)*; nirodha *(suppress)*; kshana *(moment in time)*; chitta *(mind-substance)*; anvayah *(link which connects the cause and effect sequence)*; nirodha *(suppress)*; parinamah *(transform)*.

10. tasya *(it)*; prasanta *(peaceful)*; vahita *(flow)*; samskarat *(repeating same image)*.

11. sarva *(all)*; arthata *(towards a particular object)*; ekagrata *(undisturbed attention on one object)*; kshaya *(diminish)*; udaya *(rising up)*; chittasya *(mind-substance)*; samadhi *(expanded states of Consciousness)*; parinamah *(transform)*.

12. santa *(subsided)*; udita *(has arisen)*; tulya *(identical)*; pratyaya *(thought process)*; chittasya *(mind-substance)*; ekagrata *(undisturbed attention on one object)*; parinamah *(transform)*.

13. etena *(by this)*; bhuta *(gross physical forms composed of the five natural elements)*; indriyeshu *(by the five senses)*; dharma *(the present visible physical form)*; lakshanah *(a moment; a particular space-time frame)*; avasthah *(in a state of frozen animation)*; parinamah *(transform)*; vyakhyatah *(are explained)*.

14. santa *(subsided)*; udita *(has risen)*; avyapadesya *(not manifested)*; dharma *(the present visible physical form)*; anupati *(follows from)*; dharmi *(the substratum of neutrons, protons and electrons)*.

15. krama *(successive manifestation)*; anyatvam *(distinctly different)*; parinama *(transformation)*; anyatve *(opposite from)*; hetuh *(due to)*.

16. parinama *(transformation)*; traya *(triad)*; samyamad *(becoming the object)*; atita *(gone beyond)*; anagata *(not yet begun to flow)*; jnanam *(accurate personal knowledge)*.

17. sabda *(has heard)*; artha *(meaning)*; pratyayanam *(thought process)*; itaretara *(with one another)*; adhyasat *(superimpose)*; samkarah *(intermixture)*; tat *(that)*; pravibhaga *(distinctions)*; samyamat *(becoming the object)*; sarva *(all)*; bhuta *(gross physical forms composed of the five natural elements)*; ruta *(any sound)*; jnanam *(accurate personal knowledge of)*.

18. samskara *(impression)*; sakshat *(seeing with own eyes)*; karanat *(activity that was the cause)*; purva *(previous)*; jati *(birth into particular species)*; jnanam *(accurate personal knowledge)*.

19. pratyayasya *(mental image)*; para *(higher)*; chitta *(mind-substance)*; jnanam *(accurate personal knowledge)*.

20. na *(not)*; cha *(and)*; tat *(that)*; salambanam *(connected with this mental exercise)*; tasya *(that)*; avishayi *(not with object)*; bhutatvat *(created of the five natural elements)*.

21. kaya *(body)*; rupa *(form)*; samyamat *(bringing the mind to rest in the object)*; tat *(that)*; grahya *(which is seen)*; sakti *(power)*; stambhe *(suspended)*; chakshuh *(the eye)*; prakasa *(illumination)*; asamprayoge *(disunite)*; antardhanam *(disappear)*.

22. etena *(by this)*; shabdadi *(sound, etc.)*; antardhanam *(disappear)*; uktam *(as previously explained)*.

23. sopakramam *(is presently manifesting in sequence)*; nirupa *(not yet formed)*; kramam *(successive manifestation)*; cha *(and)*;

karma *(sum of actions and results);* tat *(they);* samyamat *(becoming the object);* aparanta *(the extreme end);* jnanam *(accurate personal knowledge);* arishtebhyo *(omens and portents);* va *(also).*

24. maitri *(friendliness);* adishu *(and so on);* balani *(strength).*

25. baleshu *(strong);* hasti *(elephant);* bala *(strength);* adini *(and others).*

26. pravritti *(outward turned mind -waves);* aloka *(shining light);* nyasat *(directing);* sukshma *(subtle);* vyavahita *(are hidden);* viprakrishta *(far distant);* jnanam *(accurate personal knowledge).*

27. bhuvana *(earth and solar system);* jnanam *(accurate personal knowledge of);* surye *(sun);* samyamat *(becoming the object).*

28. chandre *(moon);* tara *(star);* vyuha *(configuration);* jnanam *(accurate personal knowledge of).*

29. dhruve *(Pole star);* tat *(that);* gati *(course);* jnanam *(accurate personal knowledge of).*

30. nabhi *(navel);* chakre *(an energy center);* kaya *(body);* vyuha *(configuration);* jnanam *(accurate personal knowledge).*

31. kantha *(throat);* kupe *(basin);* kshut *(hunger);* pipasa *(thirst);* nivrittih *(without mind-waves).*

32. kurma *(tortoise);* nadyam *(subtle nerve channel);* sthairyam *(motionless).*

33. murdha *(forehead)*; jyotishi *(effulgent light)*; siddha *(perfect in power)*; darsanam *(direct vision)*.

34. pratibhad *(divine supernormal perception)*; va *(and)*; sarvam.*(all)*.

35. hridaye *(heart)*; chitta *(mind-substance)*; samvit *(will understand and feel)*.

36. sattva *(electronic qualities of illumination, harmony and joy)* purushayoh *(true immortal self)*; atyanta *(surpassing)*; asamkirnayoh *(do not intermingle)*; pratyaya *(thought process)*; aviseshah *(not different, distinct or special)*; bhogah *(experiences of physical and emotional pleasure and pain)*.; para *(higher)*; arthat *(purpose)*; svartha *(own purpose)*; samyamat *(becoming the object)*; purusha *(true immortal self)*; jnanam *(accurate personal knowledge)*.

37. tatah *(from then on)*; pratibha *(divine supernormal perception)*; sravana *(hear)*; vedana *(touch)*; adarsa *(see)*; asvada *(taste)*; varta *(smell)*; jayante *(birth)*.

38. te *(these)*; samadhav *(expanded states of consciousness)*; upasarga *(eclipse)*; vyutthane *(outward pursuing)*; siddhayah *(supernormal powers of perfection)*.

39. bandha *(bondage)*; karana *(the activity that caused)*; shaithilyat *(relax, loosen)*; prachara *(going forth)*; samvedanat *(with knowing, perception, & sensation)*; cha *(and)*; chittasya *(of the mind-substance)*; para *(higher)*; sarira *(solid body matter)*; avesah *(penetrate)*.

40. udana *(up prana)*; jayat *(mastery)*; jala *(water)*; panka *(mud)*; kantaka *(thorns)*; adishu *(and so on)*; asangah *(not join together)*; utkrantih *(float above)*; cha *(and)*.

41. samana *(digesting prana)*; jayat *(mastery)*; jvalanam *(blazing radiance)*.

42. srotra *(hearing)*; akasayoh *(with ether of space)*; sambandha *(bind together)*; samyamat *(becoming the object)*; divyam *(divine)*; srotram *(sound)*.

43. kaya *(body)*; akasayoh *(ether of space)*; sambandha *(bind together)*; samyamat *(becoming the object)*; laghu *(weightless)*; tula *(cotton fluff)*; samapatteh *(fusion with)*; cha *(and)*; akasa *(ether of space)*; gamanam *(pass through)*.

44. bahir *(external)*; akalpita *(not imagined)*; vrittir *(thought-wave)*; maha *(great)*; videha *(out of body)*; tatah *(then)*; prakasa *(illumination)*; avarana *(covering)*; kshayah *(diminish)*.

45. sthula *(gross matter)*; svarupa *(own form)*; sukshma *(subtle)*; anvaya *(link which connects cause and effect sequence)*; arthavattva *(the significance of)*; samyamat *(becoming the object)*; bhuta *(gross physical forms composed of the five natural elements)*; jayah *(mastery)*.

46. tatha *(from then on)*; animadi *(minuteness)*; pradur *(revealed)*; bhavah *(be born)*; kaya *(body)*; sampad *(turn out well)*; tat *(that)*; dharma *(present visible physical form)*; anabhighatah *(will not disturb)*; cha *(and)*.

47. rupa *(form)*; lavanya *(graceful)*; bala *(strong)*; vajra *(energetic)*; samhananatvani *(dispel, remove, destroy)*; kaya *(body)*; sampat *(encounter)*.

48. grahana *(the process of cognition)*; svarupa *(own form)*; asmita *(I am this)*; anvaya *(link which connects cause and effect sequence)*; arthavattva *(the significance of)*; samyamat *(becoming the object)*; indriya *(senses)*; jayah *(mastery)*.

49. tato *(from this)*; mano *(lower sensory mind)*; javitvam *(swift)*; vikarana *(independent of instruments)*; bhavah *(come into being)*; pradhana *(most excellent)*; jayah *(mastery)*; cha *(and)*.

50. sattva *(electron of illumination, harmony &joy)*; purusha *(true-self)*; anyata *(different)*; khyati *(awareness)*; matrasya *(sum total)*; sarva *(all)*; bhava *(come into being)*; adhi *(supreme)*; shthatritvam *(unwavering authority)*; sarva *(all)*; jnatritvam *(knowingness)*; cha *(and)*.

51. tad *(that)*; vairagyat *(with no emotional agitation)*; api *(also)*; dosha *(bondage)*; bija *(seed)*; kshaye *(diminishes)*; kaivalyam *(separated)*.

52. sthany *(high permanent position)*; upanimantrane *(having been invited)*; sanga *(association with others)*; smaya *(smile with pride and arrogance)*; akaranam *(external expression furnishing clue to disposition of the mind)*; punah *(as virtuous)*; anishta *(ominous)*; prasangat *(evil inclination)*.

53. kshana *(moment)*; tat *(that)*; kramayoh *(successive manifestation)*; samyamat *(becoming the object)*; vivekajam *(analysis born of discrimination)*; jnanam *(accurate personal knowledge)*.

54. jati *(birth into a particular species)*; lakshana *(the particular space-time frame in which it is seen)*; desair *(position in space)*; anyata *(difference)*; anavachchhedat *(cannot be distinguished between)*; tulyayoh *(exactly the same)*; tatah *(then)*; pratipattih *(separate what had become fused together).*

55. tarakam *(cross over)*; sarva *(all)*; vishayam *(objects of the senses composed of neutrons, protons & electrons)*; sarvatha *(every aspect of)*; vishayam *(objects of the senses composed of neutrons, protons & electrons)*; akramam *(without sequence)*; cha *(and)*; iti *(thus)*; vivekajam *(analysis born of discrimination)*; jnanam *(accurate personal knowledge).*

56. sattva *(electronic quality of balance, happiness and illumination)*; purushayoh *(true-self)*; suddhi *(purity)*; samye *(become equal)*; kaivalya *(separated).*

Chapter Four

1. janma *(births)*; aushadhi *(medicinal herb)*; mantra *(a sacred divine name)*; tapah *(self-discipline)*; samadhi *(expanded consciousness)*; jah *(born)*; siddhayah *(supernormal powers of perfection)*.

2. jati *(birth in a particular species)*; antara *(another)*; parinamah *(transform)*; prakriti *(basic matter of nature)*; apurat *(flows forth into)*.

3. nimittam *(which is performed)*; aprayojakam *(not directly effected)*; prakritinam *(basic matter of nature)*; varana *(obstruction)*; bhedah *(break open)*; tu *(but)*; tatah *(from that)*; kshetrikavat *(like a farmer in his field)*.

4. nirmana *(built)*; chittani *(in the mind-substance)*; asmita *(I am all of this)*; matrat *(unit of measure)*.

5. pravritti *(outward turned mind-waves)*; bhede *(make different)*; prayojakam *(director)*; chittam *(mind-substance)*; ekam *(one)*; anekesham *(of the innumerable)*.

6. tatra *(of these)*; dhyana *(meditation)*; jam *(born of)*; anasayam *(not infect)*.

7. karma *(sum of actions and results)*; ashukla *(not white)*; akrishnam *(not black)*; yoginah *(those who are practicing the disciplines of yoga)*; trividham *(three kinds)*; itaresham *(for others)*.

8. tatah (of these); tat (that); vipaka (ripen); anugunanam (connected with one's natural tendencies); eva (also); abhivyaktih (act out); vasananam (habits, feelings, desires and fears that cause rebirth).

9. jati (birth into a particular species); desa (location); kala (time); vyavahitanam (hidden); apy (also); anantaryam (uninterrupted); smriti (memory); samskarayoh (these recorded impressions); eka (one); rupatvat (form of substance).

10. tasam (these); anaditvam (without beginning); cha (and); asishah (rest on); nityatvat (eternal principles).

11. hetu (cause); phala (effect); asraya (basis); alambanaih (that which connects a sensation with its cause); samgrihitatvat (held together); esham (these); abhave (disappear); tat (that); abhavah (disappear).

12. atita (gone beyond); anagatam (not yet begun to flow); svarupatah (own form); asty (exists); adhva (road traveled); bhedat (make different); dharmanam (present visible physical form).

13. te (they); vyakta (develop); sukshmah (subtle); gunatmanah (the nature of the qualities of the three subatomic particles in the mind).

14. parinama (transform); ekatvat (one by one); vastu (any existing thing); tattvam (level of manifestation).

15. vastu (anything that exists); samye (become equal); chitta (mind substance); bhedat (make different); tayoh (their); vibhaktah (distinct from); panthah (degree of perception).

16. na (not); cha (and); eka (one); chitta (mind-substance); tantram (depends on); vastu (anything that exists); tat (that); apramanakam (not understand correctly); tada (then); kim (what); syat (happen)..

17. tat *(that);* uparaga *(the way it becomes understood);* apekshitvat *(dependent upon);* chittasya *(mind-substance);* vastu *(anything that exists);* jnata *(accurate personal knowledge);* ajnatam *(lack of accurate personal knowledge).*

18. sada *(always);* jnatah *(accurate personal knowledge);* chitta *(mind-substance);* vrittayah *(thought-waves);* tat *(that);* prabhoh *(Lord);* purushasya *(true-self);* aparinamitvat *(uneffected by).*

19. na *(not);* tat *(that);* sva *(own);* abhasam *(luminous);* drisyatvat *(that which is seen).*

20. eka *(one);* samaye *(to regulate);* cha *(and);* ubhaye *(both);* anava *(not possible to);* dharanam *(concentrate on).*

21. chitta *(mind-substance);* antara *(internal);* drisye *(seen);* buddhibuddheh *(lense of the mind which perceives the lense of another mind);* atiprasangha *(diffuse inclinations);* smriti *(memory);* samkarah *(confused co-mingling);* cha *(and).*

22. chiteh *(pure consciousness);* aprati *(not become mixed);* samkramayah *(with sequential occurrences);* tat *(that);* akarapattau *(not bound through states of relationship);* sva *(own);* buddhi *(lense of the mind);* samvedanam *(faculty of understanding).*

23. drashtri *(the seer);* drisya *(the seen);* uparaktam *(colored by);* chittam *(mind-substance);* sarva *(all);* artham *(objects).*

24. tat *(that);* asamkhyeya *(innumerable);* vasanabhih *(habits, feelings, desires and fears that cause rebirth);* chittam *(mind-substance);* api *(also);* para *(higher);* artham *(objects);* samhatya *(co-acts in association with);* karitvat *(caused to be done).*

25. visesha *(distinctly different and special);* darsina *(direct vision of the deity);* atma *(true eternal self);* bhava *(become);* bhavana *(be born);* vi *(completely);* nivrittih *(without mind-waves).*

26. tada *(then)*; hi *(surely)*; viveka *(analysis)*; nimnam *(incline inwards)*; kaivalya *(separation)*; prag *(intelligent mode of action)*; bharam *(carrying)*; chittam *(mind-substance)*.

27. tach *(it)*; chhidreshu *(intervals between)*; pratyaya *(thought process)*; antarani *(inner psychological obstacles)*; samskare *(impressions)*; bhyah *(by the force of)*.

28. hanam *(remove)*; esham *(these)*; klesavad *(psychological causes of suffering)*; uktam *(as previously explained)*.

29. prasam *(purified and rendered clear)*; khyane *(awareness)*; apy *(also)*; akusidasya *(total disinterest)*; sarvatha *(in all respects)*; viveka *(analyze)*; khyateh *(aware of)*; dharma *(present visible physical form)*; meghah *(cloud)*; samadhih *(expanded states of consciousness)*.

30. tatah *(then)*; klesa *(psychological causes of suffering)*; karma *(cause and effect)*; nivrittih *(mind-waves cease to exist)*.

31. tada *(then)*; sarva *(all)*; avarana *(covering)*; mala *(limitations)*; apetasya *(departed)*; jnanasya *(accurate personal knowledge)*; anantyat *(without end)*; jneyam *(can be accurately known)*; alpam *(very little)*.

32. tatah *(then)*; krita *(fulfilled)*; arthanam *(purpose)*; parinama *(transform)*; krama *(sequence)*; samaptih *(reach the end, merge and terminate)*; gunanam *(three sub atomic particles)*.

33. kshana *(moment)*; pratiyogi *(dependent existence)*; parinama *(transform)*; aparanta *(the end state)*; nirgrayah *(has ceased to be known)*; kramah *(sequence)*.

34. purusha *(embodied true self)*; artha *(purpose)*; sunyanam *(void of)*; gunanam *(the three sub atomic particles)*; pratiprasavah *(reverse back into original state)*; kaivalyam *(separated)*; svarupa *(own form)*; pratishtha *(rest in)*; va *(and)*; chiti *(pure consciousness)*; sakteh *(power)*; iti *(thus)*.

✿

Glossary

a	II: 28	up
abhasam	IV: 19	luminuous
abhav(a)(ah)(at) (e)	I: 10,29; II: 25; IV: 11	not born, not exist, disappear
abhibhava	III: 9	overpower
abhijatasya	I: 41	transparent, colorless
abhimata	I: 39	that which one holds most dear
abhinivesah	II: 3,9	tenacious determination to achieve this purpose
abhivyaktih	IV: 8	act out, display, make evident
abhyantara	II: 50,51	internal
abhyasa(h)	I: 12,13,18,32	practice to form the habit
adarsa	III: 37	see
adhi	III: 50	supreme
adhigamah	I: 29	attain
adhimatra(h) (tvat)	I: 22; II: 34	intense
adhva	IV: 12	which road one is traveling
adhyasat	III: 17	superimpose
adhyatma	I: 47	essence of one's own True-Self
adini	III: 25	and others
adishu	III: 24,40	and so on
adrishta	II: 12	not seen
agama	I: 7	scriptural verification
ahimsa	II: 30,35	do not be violent, angry or aggressive
ajna(na)(tam)	II: 34; IV: 17	lack of accurate personal knowledge
akalpita	III: 44	not imagined
akaranam	III: 52	external expression furnishing clue to disposition of the mind
akarapattau	IV: 22	not bound through states of relationships
akasa(yoh)	III: 42,43	ether of space
aklishtah	I: 5	not produce suffering
akramam	III: 55	without sequence
akrishnam	IV: 7	not black
akshepi	II: 51	transcend
akusidasya	IV: 29	total disinterest

alabdha	I: 30	not gain
alambana(ih)(m)	I: 10,38; IV: 11	sensation connected with its cause, that which connects a sensation with its cause
alasya	I: 30	laziness
alinga	I: 45	undifferentiated
alingani	II: 19	without qualities
aloka	III: 26	shining light
alpam	IV: 31	very little
anabhighatah	II:.48; III: 46	will not disturb
anaditvam	IV: 10	without beginning
anagata(m)	II: 16; III: 16; IV: 12	not yet begun to flow
ananda	I: 17	Divine bliss
ananta	II: 34,47	endless
anantaryam	IV: 9	uninterrupted
anantyat	IV: 31	without end
anasayam	IV: 6	not infect
anashtam	II: 22	not destroyed
anatmasu	II: 5	corporeal body destitute of spirit
anava	I: 30; IV: 20	not possible
anavachchedat	I: 26; III: 54	cannot distinguish between
anavachchinnah	II: 31	unbounded
anekesham	IV: 5	of the innumerable
anga(m)(me)(ni)	I: 31; II: 28,29; III: 7,8	steps, parts
animadi	III: 46	minuteness
anishta	III: 52	ominous
anitya	II: 5	not eternal
anjanata	I: 41	takes that coloring
anta	I: 40	end
antardhanam	III: 21,22	disappear
antara	III: 7; IV: 2,21	another; internal
antara(ni)(ya)(yah)	I: 29,30; IV: 27	inner psychological obstacles
anu	I: 40	most minute

anubhuta	I: 11	connected with the five natural elements
anugamat	I: 17	connected with
anugunanam	IV: 8	connected to one's natural tendencies
anukara	II: 54	resembles
anumana	I: 7,49	logical conclusion
anumoditah	II: 34	approve of it
anupasyah	II: 20	appears to be
anupati	I: 9; III: 14	following upon
anusayi	II: 7,8	consequence of
anushasanam	I: 1	instruction
anushravika	I: 15	heard about
anushthanat	II: 28	by carrying out
anuttamah	II: 42	unsurpassed
anvaya(h)	III: 9,45,48	link which connects cause and effect sequence
anya(h)(ta)	I: 18,49,50; II: 22; III: 50,54	different
anyatvam	III: 15	distinctly different
anyatve	III: 15	opposite from
apara	I: 24	beyond
aparanta	III: 23; IV: 33	the extreme end, the end state
aparigraha(h)	II: 30,39	renounce amassing possessions and accepting gifts with strings attached
aparinamitvat	IV: 18	uneffected by
apavarga	II: 18	emancipation from bodily existence
apekshitvat	IV: 17	dependent upon
apetasya	IV: 31	departed
apramanakam	IV: 16	not understand correctly
aprati	IV: 22	not become mixed
aprayojakam	IV: 3	not directly effects
apunya	I: 33; II: 14	evil, vice
apurat	IV: 2	flows forth, evolves
apy	IV: 9,29	also
arishtebhyo	III: 23	omens & portents

artha(h)(m)	I: 28,32,42,43; II: 2,18,21,22; III: 17; IV: 23,24,34	meaning, purpose,cause; a thing, an object
arthamatra	III: 3	the height, depth, breadth, length
artha(nam)(t)	III: 36; IV: 32	purpose
arthata	III: 11	towards a particular object
arthatvat	I: 49	its true meaning
arthavattva	III: 45,48	the significance of
asamkhyeya	IV: 24	innumerable
asamkirnayoh	III: 36	do not intermingle
asampramoshah	I: 11	not forgotten
asamprayog(a)(e)	II: 54; III: 21	sever the link, disunite
asamsargah	II: 40	will not want contact with
asana(m)	II: 29,46	sitting posture
asangah	III: 40	not join together
asannah	I: 21	soon
asaya(h)(ir)	I: 24; II: 12	stored
asevitah	I: 14	persistence
ashta	II: 29	eight
ashukla	IV: 7	not white
asishah	IV: 10	rest on
asmita	I: 17; II: 3,6; III: 48; IV: 4	I am this
asraya(tvam)	II: 36; IV: 11	basis
asteya	II: 30,37	do not steal
asty	IV: 12	exists
asuchi	II: 5	not pure
asuddhi	II: 28,43	impurities
asvada	III: 37	taste
asya	I: 40	one
atad	I: 8	not that
atha	I: 1	now
atiprasangha	IV: 21	diffuse inclinations
atisayam	I: 25	excelled
atita	III: 16; IV: 12	gone beyond

atma	II: 5,21,41; IV: 25	true-self, true-eternal-self
atmakam	II: 18	consisting of
atyanta	III: 36	surpassing
aushadhi	IV: 1	medicinal herb
avarana(m)	II: 52; III: 44, IV: 31	covering
avasthah	III: 13	in a state of frozen animation
avasthanam	I: 3	remains in and exhibits
avesah	III: 39	penetrate
avidya	II: 3,4,5,24	ignorance
aviplava	II: 26	unwavering
avirati	I: 30	not abstaining
avisesha(h)	II: 19; III: 36	not different, distinct or special
avishayi	III: 20	not an object
avyapadesya	III: 14	not manifested
ayuh	II: 13	life span
badhane	II: 33	disturbing
bah(ir)(ya)	II: 50,51; III: 8,44	outer, external
bal(a)(ani)(eshu)	III: 24,25,47	strength, strong
bandha(h)	III: 1,39	bondage, bind
bhara(m)	I: 48; IV: 26	bearing, carrying
bhaumah	II: 31	a level, belonging to a state
bhava(h)(na)(nam) (natah)(u)	I: 19,28,33,; II: 2,33,34; III: 9,46,49,50; IV: 25	birth, come into being, become, be born
bhed(ah)(at)(e)	IV: 3,5,12,15	break open, make different, modify
bhoga(h)	II: 13,18; III: 36	experience of physical and emotional pleasure and pain
bhranti	I: 30	distorted
bhumi(h)(katva)	I: 14,30; II: 27	become grounded
bhumishu	III: 6	in stages
bhuta	II: 18; III: 13,17,45	gross physical forms composed of the five natural elements
bhutatvat	III: 20	created of the five natural elements
bhuvah	I: 31	accompany

bhuvana	III: 27	earth and solar system
bhyah	III: 7	from
bija(m)	I: 25; III: 51	seed
brahmacharya	II: 30,38	do not lust over others; continence
buddhi	IV: 22	lense of the mind
buddhibuddheh	IV: 21	lense of the mind which perceives the lense of another mind
chakre	III: 30	chakra, an energy center
chakshuh	III: 21	the eye
chandre	III: 28	moon
chaturthah	II: 51	has been explained
chetana	I: 29	divine counsciousness
chhidreshu	IV: 27	intervals between
chit(eh)(i)	IV: 22,34	pure consciousness
chitta(m)(ni)(sya)	I: 2,30,33,37; II: 54; III: 1,9,11,12,19,35,39; IV: 4,5,15,16 - 18,21,23,24,26	mind-substance, mind
dars(ana)(anam)(ina)	I: 30; II: 6,41; III: 33; IV: 25	direct vision of the deity
daurmanasya	I: 31	despair, anxiety, bad disposition
desa(ir)	II: 31,50; III: 1,54; IV: 9	location, place, position in space
dharana(m)(su)	II: 29,53; III: 1; IV: 20	concentration
dharma(nam)	III: 13,14,46; IV: 12,29	the present visible physical form
dharmi	III: 14	the substratum of neutrons, protons andelectrons
dhruve	III: 29	Pole Star
dhyana(m)(t)	I: 39; II: 11,29; III: 2; IV: 6	meditation
diptih	II: 28	light
dirgha	I: 14; II: 50	long
divyam	III: 42	divine
dosha	III: 51	bondage
drasht(a)(ri)	II: 17,20; IV: 23	one who sees
drashtuh	I: 3	wishing or desiring to see
dridha	I: 14	unwavering
drig	II: 6	seeing, viewing, looking at

driseh	II: 25	seen, beheld
drishta	I: 15; II: 12	looked at, beheld, perceived
drisimatrah	II: 20	the amount that is seen
drisya	IV: 23	the seen
drisya(m)(sya)	II: 18,21	having seen; visible; conspicuous
drisy(atvat)	II: 17; IV: 19,21	that sees, seen
(ayoh)(e)		
duhk(am)(ha)	I: 31,33; II:	pain & suffering, unhappiness
(hair)(ham)	5,8,15,16,34	
dvandva	II: 48	opposites
dvesha(h)	II: 3,8	mental excitement and passionate emotional agitation due to aversions to certain things
eka	I: 32; III: 2; IV: 9,16,20	first; one
ekagrata	III: 11,12	undisturbed attention on one object
ekagrya	II: 41	closely attentive
ekam	IV: 5	one
ekatmata	II: 6	blend together as one identity
ekatra	III: 4	one after one
ekatvat	IV: 14	uniform
esham	IV: 11,28	these
et(aya)(ena)	I: 44; III: 13,22	by this
eva	I: 46; II: 15,21; III: 3; IV: 8	also
gamanam	III: 43	pass through
gati	II: 49; III: 29	movement, course
grahana	I: 41; III: 48	act of knowing, the process of cognition
grahitri	I: 41	knower
grahya	III: 21	which is known
grayeshu	I: 41	that which is known
guna(nam)	I: 16; II: 15,19; IV: 32,34	the three sub atomic particles
gunatmanah	IV: 13	the nature of the qualities of the three sub atomic particles in the mind
guru	I: 26	bringer of enlightenment, spiritual master
hana(m)	II: 25,26; IV: 28	remove
hasti	III: 25	elephant
hetu(h)(r)	II: 17,23,24; III: 15; IV: 11	cause, due to
hetutvat	II: 14	will produce
heya(h)(m)(s)	II: 10,11,16,17	refuse to accept

Glossary

hi	IV: 26	surely
himsadayah	II: 34	violence done by oneself
hlada	II: 14	cooling, refreshing, delightful
hridaye	III: 35	heart
indri(a)(ya)	II: 18,41,43,54,	senses
(yanam)(yeshu)	55; III: 13,48	
ishtadevata	II: 44	one's chosen form of God
isvara(h)	I: 23,24; II:	divine being
	1,32,45	
itaratra	I: 4	at other times
itaresham	I: 20; IV: 7	by others
itaretara	III: 17	with one another
iva	I: 41, 43; II:	as if, like
	6,54; III: 3	
jah	IV: 1	born
jala	III: 40	water
jam	IV: 6	born of
janma	II: 12,39; IV: 1	lives, births
japah	I: 28	repetition of a name of God
jati	II: 13,31; III:	a particular birth
	18,54; IV: 2,9	
javitvam	III: 49	swiftly
jaya(h)	II: 41; III:	victory, mastery
	45,48,49	
jayante	III: 37	birth
jayat	III: 5,40,41	mastery
jayatva	I: 31	uncontrolled
jna	I: 25	knowing
jna(na)(nam)	I: 8,9,38,42; II:	accurate personal knowledge
(nasya)(ta)(tah)	28; III: 16 -	
	19,23,26-	
	30,36,53,55;	
	IV:17,18,31	
jnatritvam	III: 50	knowingness
jneyam	IV: 31	can be accurately known
jugupsa	.II: 40	indifferent
jvalanam	III: 41	blazing radiance
jyotishi	III: 33	effulgent light
jyotishmati	I: 36	effulgent light of your Divine Self
kaivalya(m)	II: 25; III:	separated
	51,56; IV: 26,34	
kala	I: 14; II: 31,50;	time
	IV: 9	
kalena	I: 26	within time

kantaka	III: 40	thorns
kantha	III: 31	throat
karana(t)	II: 2; III: 18,39	the activity that caused
karit(a)(vat)	II: 34; IV: 24	cause to be done
karma	I: 24; II: 12; III: 23; IV: 7,30	cause and effect, sum of actions and results
karuna	I: 33	compassion
kathamta	II: 39	answers how and why
kaya	II: 43; III: 21,30, 43,46,47	body
khya(ne)(teh) (ter)(ti)(tih)	I: 16; II: 26,28; III: 50; IV: 29	aware of
khyatir	II: 5	the idea
klesa(h)(vad)	I: 24; II: 2,3,12; IV: 28,30	psychological causes of suffering
klishta	I: 5	mental and emotional suffering
krama(h)(am) (yoh)	III: 15,23,53; IV: 32,33	successive manifestation, orderly progression, sequence
krita	II: 22,34; IV: 32	fulfill, accomplish, achieve
kriya	II: 1,18,36	motion, activity
krodha	II: 34	anger
kshana	III: 9,53; IV: 33	moment, moment in time
kshay(a)(ah)(at) (e)	II: 28,43; III: 11,44,51	diminish, decrease
kshetram	II: 4	field
kshetrikavat	IV: 3	like a farmer in his field
kshina	I: 41	weaken
kshiyati	II: 52	dissolve
kshut	III: 31	hunger
kupe	III: 31	basin
kurma	III: 32	tortoise
labhah	II: 38,42	gain
laghu	III: 43	weightless
lakshana(h)	III: 13,54	a particular space-time frame
lavanya	III: 47	graceful
layanam	I: 19	merge
linga	II: 19	with qualities
lobha	II: 34	greed
lokah	III: 5	shining forth
madhya	I: 22; II: 34	moderate
maha	II: 31; III: 44	great
mahattva	I: 40	most great
maitri	I: 33; III: 24	friendliness

mala	IV: 31	limitations, physical or moral impurities
manasah	I: 35; II: 53	the mind
maner	I: 41	jewel
mano	III: 49	lower sensory mind
mantra	IV: 1	a sacred divine name
matra(sya)(t)	I: 43; II: 19; III: 50; IV: 4	sum total, unit of measure
meghah	IV: 29	cloud
mithya	I: 8	false
moha	II: 34	delusion
mridu	I: 22; II: 34	mild
mrishtah	I: 24	mortality
mudita	I: 33	rejoicing
mul(ah)(e)	II: 12,13	root
murdha	III: 33	forehead
nabhi	III: 30	navel
nadyam	III: 32	subtle nerve channel
nairantarya	I: 14	without interruption or interval
nashtam	II: 22	destroyed
nibandhani	I: 35	that which binds
nidra	I: 6,10,38	deep dreamless sleep
nimittam	IV: 3	which is performed
nimnam	IV: 26	incline inwards
nir	I: 25	not is
nirbhasa(m)	I: 43; III: 3	shines forth
nirbijah	I: 51	without seeds
nirbijasya	III: 8	in relation to seedless
nirgrahyah	IV: 33	has ceased to be known
nirmana	IV: 4	built, constructed
nirodh(a)(ah)(an)(e)	I: 2,12,51; III: 9	suppress
nirupa	III: 23	not yet formed
nirvichara	I: 44,47	without reflective comtemplation
nirvitarka	I: 43	without logical examination
nitya	II: 5	eternal
nityatvat	IV: 10	eternal principles
nivrittih	III: 31; IV: 25,30	without mind waves; mind waves cease to exist
niyama(h)	II: 29,32	observances, five virtues for happy personal life
nyasat	III: 26	directing, applying
om	I: 27	sound of the instant of creation
pancha	I: 5	five

panka	III: 40	mud
panthah	IV: 15	degree of perception
para	III: 19,36,39; IV: 24	higher, beyond
paraih	II: 40	distant
param(a)	I: 16,40; II: 55	highest, most exalted
paridrishto	II: 50	regulated
parinama(h)	II: 15; III: 9,11 - 13,15,16; IV: 2,14,32,33	transformation, change
parisuddhau	I: 43	ultimate state of purity
paritapa	II: 14	hot, tormenting, difficult
parvani	II: 19	stages of development
paryavasanam	I: 45	beyond impressions that produce rebirth
phala(h)	II: 14,34,36; IV: 11	result, effect, fruit of
pipasa	III: 31	thirst
prabhoh	IV: 18	Lord
prachara	III: 39	going forth
prachchhardana	I: 34	controlled exhalation
pradhana	III: 49	most excellent
pradur	III: 9,46	visible, revealed
prag	IV: 26	intelligent mode of action
prajna	I: 20,48,49; II: 27; III: 5	enlightened intelligence & wisdom
prakasa	II: 18,52; III: 21,44	illumination
prakriti(nam)	I: 19; IV: 2,3	the basic matter of nature, out of which evolves the universe;the highest and most subtle form of the universe;the original material substance
pramada	I: 30	disinterest
pramana(ni)	I: 6,7	correct understanding
pranasya	I: 34	of the breath
pranavah	I: 27	pronouncement; sound of the moment of creation, the Om
pranayama	II: 29,49	breath control
pranidhana(ni)(t)	I: 23; II: 1,32,45	mentally and emotionally surrendered to and focused on
pranta	II: 27	last
prasada(h)(nam)	I: 33,47	clarity, clear, pleasant
prasam	IV: 29	purified and rendered clear
prasangat	III: 52	evil inclination
prasanta	III: 10	peaceful

prasupta	II: 4	dormant
prasvasa	I: 31	uncontrolled exhalation
prasvasayor	II: 49	controlled exhalation
prati	II: 22	by reversing
pratibandhi	I: 50	obstructs & prevents
pratibha(d)	III: 34,37	divine supernormal perception
pratipaksha	II: 33,34	prevent by reversing to the opposite
pratipattih	III: 54	reversing and seperating what had become fused together
pratiprasava(h)	II: 10; IV: 34	reverse back into original state
pratishedha	I: 32	counteract, oppose
pratishtha(m) (yam)	I: 8; II: 35-38; IV: 34	rest in, stand still in
pratiyogi	IV: 33	dependent existence
pratyahara(h)	II: 29,54	turning the senses inward; voluntary sensory deprivation
pratyak(sha)	I: 7,29	direct inner perception
pratyaya(h)(nam)	I: 10,18,19; II: 20; III: 2,12, 17,36; IV: 27	thought process
pratyayasya	III: 19	mental image, belief
pravibhaga	III: 17	distinction, differentiation
pravritti(h)	I: 35; III: 26; IV: 5	outward turned mindwaves
prayatna	II: 47	willful effort
prayojakam	IV: 5	director
punah	III: 52	as if virtuous
punya	I: 33; II: 14	virtuous
purusha(sya) (yoh)	I: 16,24; III: 36,50,56; IV: 18,34	true-self, true immortal self, embodied true-self, consciousness embodied as man
purv(a)(ah)(e)	I: 18; III: 7,18	previous
purvakah	I: 20; II: 34	precede
purvesham	I: 26	former
raga(h)	I: 37; II: 3,7	mental excitement and passionate emotional agitation due to desires for certain things
ratna	II: 37	jewels
ritam	I: 48	supreme undiluted truth regarding divine universal laws
rudho	II: 9	implanted
rupa	I: 8; III: 21,47	form
rupatvat	IV: 9	form of substance
ruta	III: 17	any sound

sabda	I: 42; III: 17	has heard
sabijah	I: 46	with seed
sada	IV: 18	always
sadharanatvat	II: 22	who are concentrated on it
saha	I: 31	natural
saithilya	II: 47	lessen
sakshat	III: 18	seeing with own eyes
sakt(eh)(i)(yoh) (yor)	II: 6,23; III: 21; IV: 34	power
salambanam	III: 20	connected with this mental excercise
sam	I: 21	with
samadh(av)(i) (ih)	I: 20,46,51; II: 2,29,45; III: 3,11,38; IV:1,29	expanded states of consciousness
samana	III: 41	digesting prana
samapatt(eh) (ibhyam)(ih)	I: 41; II: 47; III: 43	will become one with; fusion with
samaptih	IV: 32	reach the end, merge and terminate
samaya	II: 31	coming together
samaye	IV: 20	to regulate, make level
sambandha	III: 42,43	bind together, relationship with
sambodhah	II: 39	perfect enlightened understanding
samgrihitatvat	IV: 11	held together, restrained
samhananatvani	III: 47	will dispel, remove, destroy
samhatya	IV: 24	co-acts in association, combined
samjna	I: 15	has recovered consciousness
samkarah	III: 17; IV: 21	intermixture; confused co-mingling
samkhyabhih	II: 50	with number
samkirna	I: 42	intermingle
samkramayah	IV: 22	with sequential occurances
samnidhau	II:.35	presence of
sampad	III: 46	turn out well
sampat	III: 47	encounter
samprajnatah	I: 17	with enlightened intelligence and wisdom
samprayogah	II: 44	will be united with
samsaya	I: 30	doubt
samskara(h)	I: 18,50; II: 15; III: 18	impression (of past event stored in the mind-substance)
samskarat	III: 10	repeating same image
samskarayoh	III: 9; IV: 9	these recorded impressions
samskare	IV: 27	impressions
samtosha(t)	II: 32,42	with contentment
samvedanam	IV: 22	faculty of understanding

samvedanat	III: 39	knowing, perception, with sensation
samvit	III: 35	will understand and feel
samyama(d)(h)(t)	III:4,16,17,21, 23,27,36,42,43, 45,48,53	becoming the object
samye	III: 56; IV: 15	become equal
samyoga(h)	II: 17,23,25	identity with, conjunction,joined to, united with
sanga	III: 52	association with others
santa	III: 12,14	subsided, ended
saptadha	II: 27	sevenfold
sarira	III: 39	solid body matter
sarupyam	I: 4	with those forms
sarva(m)	I: 25,51; II: 15, 31,37; III: 11,17, 34,50,55; IV: 23,31	all
sarvatha	III: 55; IV: 29	every aspect of; in all respects
sati	II: 13,49	exist
satkara	I: 14	positive attitude, respect, reverence
sattva	II: 41; III: 36,50,56	electron; the qualities of illumination, harmony and joy, light and peace
satya	II: 30,36	truthfulness; do not lie
saucha(t)	II: 32,40	by attaining purity
saumanasya	II: 41	cheerful mind
savichara	I: 44	with reflective contemplation
savitarka	I: 42	with logical examination
seshah	I: 18	undefiled
shabda	I: 9	heard
shabdadi	III: 22	sound
shaithilyat	III: 39	loosen
shthatritvam	III: 50	unwavering authority
shudda	II: 20	pure and clear
shunyo	I: 9	void
siddha	III: 33	perfect in power
siddh(ayah)(i) (ir)	II: 43,45; III: 38; IV: 1	supernormal powers, powers of perfection
silam	II: 18	qualities
smaya	III: 52	smile with pride and arrogance
smrit(ayah)(i) (ih)	I: 6,11,20,43; IV: 9,21	memory
sopakramam	III: 23	presently manifesting in sequence
sraddha	I: 20	faith, devotion, surrender, enthusiasm
sravana	III: 37	hear

srotra	III: 42	hearing
srotram	III: 42	sound
sruta	I: 49	heard
stamb(ah)(he)	II: 50; III: 21	stop, suspend
sthairy(am)(e)	II: 39; III: 32	motionless
sthany	III: 52	high permanent position
sthi(ra)(tatvani)	I: 13,30,35;	steady, still
(tau)(ti)	II: 18,46	
sthula	III: 45	gross matter
styana	I: 30	resistance
suchi	II: 5	pure
suddhi	II: 41; III: 56	purity
sukha(m)	I: 33; II: 5,7,42,46	happy
sukshma(h)	I: 44,45; II: 10,50; III: 26,45; IV: 13	subtle
sunya(m)(nam)	I: 43; III: 3; IV: 34	void
surye	III: 27	sun
sva	II: 23; III: 45; IV: 19,22	own
svadhyaya(d)	II: 1,32,44	meditation on one's own mind
svami	II: 23	owner, master
svanga	II: 40	parts of one's own body
svapna	I: 38	dream
svarasa	II: 9	innate love of pleasure
svartha	III: 36	own purpose
svarup(a)(atah) (e)	I: 3,43; II: 23,54; III: 3,45, 48; IV: 12,34	own form
svasa	I: 31; II: 49	inhalation
syat	IV: 16	happen
tajjah	I: 50	of that born
tanata	III: 2	unbroken, continuous
tantram	IV: 16	depends on
tanu	II: 2,4	reduce, weaken
tapa(h)(sah)	II: 1,15,32,43; IV:1	heat, to burn up, to melt down and purify, self-imposed discipline, tormenting
tara	III: 28	star
tarakam	III: 55	cross-over
tatstha	I: 41	rests in that

tattva(m)	I: 32; IV: 14	a level of the matter of the universe, a category of matter
tayyah	I: 5	types, kinds
tivra	I: 21	ardent
traya	III: 16	triad
trayam	III: 4,7	these three
trividham	IV: 7	three kinds
tula	III: 43	cotton fluff
tulya	III: 12	identical
tulyayoh	III: 54	exactly the same
tyagah	II: 35	abandon
ubhaye	IV: 20	both
udana	III: 40	up prana
udaranam	II: 4	active, energetic
udaya	III: 11	rising up
udita	III: 12,14	has arisen, ascended
uktam	III: 22; IV: 28	as previously explained
upalabdhi	II: 23	the appearance of, superimposed condition
upanimantrane	III: 52	having been invited
uparaga	IV: 17	the way it is colored, the way it is understood
uparaktam	IV: 23	colored by
upasarga	III: 38	eclipse
upasthanam	II: 37	abide with, approach, appear
upayah	II: 26	the means, the method
upekshanam	I: 33	non-attached empathy
utkrantih	III: 40	float above, levitate
utpanna	I: 35	rise above
uttaresham	II: 4	for the others
vachakah	I: 27	the word or sound which was expressed
vahi(ta)	II: 9; III: 10	flows
vaira	II: 35	conflict
vairagya(m)(t)	I: 12,15; III: 51	emotionally free from the aggitation and suffering caused by desire and fear
vaisaradye	I: 47	brightness that reflects the wholeness of parts
vaitrishnyam	I: 16	not thirst
vajra	III: 47	energetic
varana	IV: 3	obstruction, mound
varta	III: 37	smell
vasana(bhih) (nam)	IV: 8,24	habits, feelings desires and fears that cause rebirth
vasikara(h)	I: 15,40	mastery over, made subject to one's will

vastu	I: 9; IV: 14-17	any existing thing
vasyata	II: 55	obedient to your will,tamed, subdued
vati	I: 35	connected to
vedana	III: 37	touch
vedaniyah	II: 12	will be experienced, felt and known
veganam	I: 21	enthusiasm
vi	IV: 25	completely
vibhaktah	IV: 15	distinct from
vichara	I: 17	reflective contemplation
vichchhedah	II: 49	that which is between, breaking, separating
vichchhinna	II: 4	intercepted
videha	I: 19; III: 44	with no body
vidharana	I: 34	maintain outside
vidusho	II: 9	defile, corrupt
vikalpa(h)(ih)	I: 6,9,42	imagination
vikarana	III: 49	independant of instruments
vikshepa(h)	I: 30,31	distraction
viniyogah	III: 6	accomplish union
vipaka(h)	I: 24; II: 13; IV: 8	ripen
viparyaya(h)	I: 6,8	incorrect understanding
viprakrishta	III: 26	far distant
virama	I: 18	terminated
virodhat	II: 15	conflict
virya	I: 20; II: 38	heroism
visesha(h)	I: 22,24,49; II: 19 IV: 25	distinctly different and special
vishaya(m)(nam)	I:11,15,33,35,37, 44,49; II: 51; III: 55	object of the senses composed of neutrons, protons & electrons
vishayatvam	I: 45	province of object of the senses
visoka	I: 36	beyond sorrow
vita	I: 37	without
vitarka	I: 17; II: 33,34	logical examination, thinking
vitrishnasya	I: 15	not thirst
viveka	II: 26,28; IV: 26,29	analysis, discrimination between true thoughts and ignorant ones
vivek(ajam) (inah)	II: 15; III: 53,55	analysis, born of discrimination
vratam	II: 31	vow
vritt(ayah)(er)(i) (ir)	I: 2,4,5,10,41; II: 11,15,50; III: 44 IV: 18	thought-waves , mind-waves

vyadhi	I: 30	illness
vyakhyata	I: 44; III: 13	explained
vyakta	IV: 13	evolve, develop
vyavahita(nam)	III: 26; IV: 9	hidden
vyuha	III: 28,30	configuration, arrangement
vyutthan(a)(e)	III: 9,38	outward pursueing
yama(h)	II: 29,30	restraints, virtues for happy relationships
yatnah	I: 13	effort
yoga(h)(s)	I: 1,2; II: 1,28	to join; yoga psychology; mystical union
yoginah	IV: 7	for those who are practicing the disciplines of yoga
yogyata	II: 53	becomes fit for mystical union
yogyatvani	II: 41	becomes capable of mystical union

Index

New Life Books publishes books and tapes on personal unfoldment and living a spiritual life in the midst of our modern world. It is our hope that doing so will help alleviate suffering and create a more peaceful world. We carry all books and tapes by Swami Savitripriya.

For a free copy of our catalogue, which lists talks and seminars; books, tapes and videos; and music tapes; please write to:

New Life Books

160 Remington Drive, Suite 147

Sunnyvale, California 94087

This book was designed and typeset on an Apple Macintosh SE , and output on an Apple Personal Laser Writer NT. The typeface is 11 point Palatino. Design by Detta Penna. Printed by McNaughton & Gunn on Finch Opaque.